CW00547477

HOPE AND LEARNING

HOPE AND LEARNING

Our Journey with Schizophrenia

LINDA SNOW-GRIFFIN, PHD

Cherish
EDITIONS

First published in Great Britain 2021 by Cherish Editions

Cherish Editions is a trading style of Shaw Callaghan Ltd & Shaw Callaghan 23 USA, INC.

The Foundation Centre

Navigation House, 48 Millgate, Newark

Nottinghamshire NG24 4TS UK

www.triggerhub.org

Text Copyright © 2021 Linda Snow-Griffin Ph.D.

All rights reserved. No part of this publication may be reproduced, stored in a re-trieval system, or transmitted in any form or by any means, electronic, mechanical, photocopying, recording or otherwise, without prior permission in writing from the publisher

British Library Cataloguing in Publication Data

A CIP catalogue record for this book is available upon request from the British Library

ISBN: 9781913615154

This book is also available in the following eBook formats:

ePUB: 9781913615161

Linda Snow-Griffin Ph.D. has asserted her right under the Copyright, Design and Patents Act 1988 to be identified as the author of this work

Cover design by Kitty Turner

Typeset by Lapiz Digital Services

Cherish Editions encourages diversity and different viewpoints; however, all views, thoughts, and opinions expressed in this book are the author's own and are not necessarily representative of Cherish Editions as an organization.

All material in this book is set out in good faith for general guidance and no liability can be accepted for loss or expense incurred in following the information given. Although the author is a trained mental health professional, this book is intended for informational purposes only and for your own personal use and guidance. It is not intended to diagnose, treat or act as a substitute for professional medical advice.

"Heartwarming, compassionate, encouraging and wise. Both scholarly and well researched and offering very concrete, practical advice on her 20-year journey. Written with courage, candor and warmth, compassion and **love**. It is a guide for anyone who knows or has a family member with schizophrenia or wants to understand what it is like to have schizophrenia or live with one who does.

This book is for every parent who worries about their child being 'different' and wondering how their son or daughter will survive when they are gone."

Lillie Weiss, Ph.D., psychologist and author of seven books, including *Therapist's Guide to Self Care*

"What a wonderful contribution to our field. *Hope and Learning, Our Journey with Schizophrenia* by Linda Snow-Griffin, Ph.D. offers the reader a unique perspective and understanding of schizophrenia. As a psychologist and parent, with a son diagnosed with schizophrenia, she shares how the various stereotypes of schizophrenia have impacted her family. The author describes the family journey with their son and realizes that, even though many advances have been made in therapeutic approaches and medication, they must continue their journey with hope and continued learning. I highly recommend this new book for all professionals who work with schizophrenia and for all individuals and families dealing with a mental illness and are on a journey. Therapists can gain unique insights that will help them deal with similar situations. References are included at the end of the book."

William C. Wester, II, Ed.D., ABPP (Co/Fam). ABPH (CI)
Psychologist, retired
Past President, State of Ohio Board of Psychology
Past President, American Society of Clinical Hypnosis

"In over 40 years of clinical practice, I have had the privilege to work with hundreds of the wonderful, strong and brave victims of schizophrenia. However, I rarely got to know their families. What is it like for a parent to learn their child has a devastating, incurable illness? Dr. Snow-Griffin gives us a unique perspective as not only a parent, but a parent who has years of training in understanding and treating schizophrenia and fully understands the hurdles her child will face in life. The way to cope with this situation cannot be taught—it must be lived. We all owe Dr. Snow-Griffin a debt of gratitude for sharing her journey."

James D. Dahmann, Ph.D.
Licensed psychologist
Past President, Cincinnati Academy of Professional Psychology
NAMI-NKY Board Member
Mental Health Consultant, Hostage Negotiation Team

"Thank you for allowing me to read your work. It provides a wealth of important information and help for struggling families. My own son did not survive schizophrenia, and this is the information and encouragement I wish we'd had when we were trying to help him. The book is aptly named; it provides a beacon of hope."

Lynda L. Crane, Ph.D.
Professor of psychology
Douglas's mom

AUTHOR BIO

Linda Snow-Griffin, Ph.D. is a retired psychologist. She is the mother of two, stepmother of three adult children and grandmother of sixteen. She has practiced in a variety of settings – college, university and community mental health – and spent the last 30 years in private practice in Cincinnati. Her desire is to provide hope to families coping with mental illness, especially schizophrenia, and to dispel misunderstandings about the illness.

This book is dedicated to Jacob and to all individuals and families who face the challenges of schizophrenia. May their journey be one of hope.

In order to protect confidentiality, all names but my own have been changed. Descriptions of some individuals have been altered to avoid identification as well. The facts and experiences of my son, husband, daughter and myself are true to our perceptions. Data about schizophrenia is research-based and referenced at the end of the book.

CONTENTS

Introduction 1

Chapter 1   What is Schizophrenia? 7
Chapter 2   A "Normal" Start.. 17
Chapter 3   Why Didn't I See This Coming? 25
Chapter 4   Mother's Guilt..37
Chapter 5   First-Year Challenges.................................. 45
Chapter 6   The College Years 55
Chapter 7   Post-College Struggles 73
Chapter 8   Coping With Schizophrenic "Leftovers"...... 85
Chapter 9   Recovery 95
Chapter 10 Family Impact of Schizophrenia.................109
Chapter 11 Fighting Stereotypes....................................123
Chapter 12 Essentials of Self-Care 139
Chapter 13 What's Next?...151

Acknowledgements 155
References 157

Turbulence is a term used in physics to describe what happens to the flow of fluid through pipes that becomes rough or volatile as a result of external forces. This same word is used to explain extremely hot plasma in reactors, wildfires in California and extreme weather patterns. Pilots use it to describe weather events that result in bumpy flights. Taming the turbulence is a scientific challenge.

What I am about to describe is how turbulence interrupted life as my family knew it and how we have spent the past 20 years trying to tame it.

INTRODUCTION

"You do not have schizophrenia," I told him. "I'm a psychologist. I would know if my own son had schizophrenia."

I had just discovered a green spiral-bound notebook on the floor of my son's disheveled bedroom, on the front of which he had written the words "My Schizophrenic Notebook".

Jacob gazed patiently at me as he tried to explain the meaning of his journal entries. He had recently completed an Introduction to Psychology class the semester before and, living with a mother who was a psychologist in private practice, already knew a lot about the subject. But still, I thought, *Schizophrenia? That couldn't possibly be...*

"But you have to have some type of hallucinations," I argued. "You have to either see things that other people don't see or hear things that other people don't hear."

"I hear voices," he said. "Numerous voices."

With more probing, he described several distinct voices that he did not feel were a part of him but that he heard on a regular basis – ones that would tell him what to say and how to act. One voice was particularly malicious and criticized him unmercifully. Another was like a video game, with a running dialogue at the bottom of a screen coaching him to interact with others in a formal, prescribed manner. He explained that at school he had begun to address friends he passed in the halls by their first and last names and had to state what the "screen" told him to say, such as, "Hello, Jason Miller. How are you today?", which must have seemed odd to his friends.

His "picture voice", meanwhile, would flash images at him, telling him what he had to do. If he disobeyed this voice, he would get headaches. I found out years later that sometimes, when he was driving, the voice would tell him to turn left into incoming traffic.

Fortunately, he said he always silenced messages of that kind and put up with the headache.

Other voices kept him emotionally distant from others and interfered with his concentration, like a room full of people vying for your attention when you are trying to focus on another competing task.

This is how our story began 20 years ago when my son was finally diagnosed by a psychologist, and later a psychiatrist, with Schizophrenia, Disorganized Type.

***

In the past, if someone were diagnosed with schizophrenia, they could expect months, if not years of hospitalizations. Personal and professional goals had to be abandoned. Life was interrupted with very little chance of a recovery. Between 1900 and 1950, prior to the discovery of the first antipsychotic medication, medical treatments were unreliable and often dangerous, such as pyrotherapy, which involved injecting strep, tuberculosis or even malaria pathogens to create a fever. Most interventions were used to control behaviors, such as coma therapies, hydrotherapies (ice-cold baths), electroshock therapies and lobotomies. With the discovery of Thorazine, psychotic symptoms improved, but the side effects of early medication were often heavy sedation, tremors and uncontrollable muscle movements.

Gradually, over the past 50 years, this picture has changed. Thanks to both medical and psychosocial research, medications and treatments have improved. In the 20 years since my son was diagnosed with schizophrenia, treatment has made even greater leaps. With the advent of the newest type of medications, many people with schizophrenia can manage and sometimes find total remission from incapacitating symptoms. New psychological approaches now use strength-based methods of assessment and treatment that work with the many aspects of a person's life that are important to recovery. Best practices now include cognitive behavioral therapy, skill-building tools, employment counseling, family education and involvement, substance-abuse intervention, and programs addressing physical healthcare. Most importantly, there has been a paradigm shift. People with schizophrenia are now active partners with psychiatrists, psychologists and other healthcare professionals in devising treatment goals and selecting interventions that will help them most.

What this means is that currently many people with schizophrenia are able to live independent and productive lives. That doesn't mean that the recovery process is easy or that everyone is able to resume life the way it was prior to the diagnosis. According to the Recovery to Practice program (American Psychological Association & Jansen, 2014), it means that most people with schizophrenia can now achieve the four goals of recovery: personal health; a stable home; a sense of purpose; and community participation and support.

Unlike many stories previously written about individuals with schizophrenia, my son has been able to benefit from the new approaches to treatment and has met recovery goals. While the Recovery to Practice approach was not accepted by all his early doctors and counselors, many of the recovery ideas began to find their way into treatments that he eventually received. The hope of recovery has been a welcome model.

When my son was first diagnosed, however, I was not prepared to hear that he had schizophrenia. Confusion, denial and panic took over. Those early moments did not even feel real. How was the best way to help him? What did he need to get better? *Could* he even get better? Embracing the thought that his illness may be lifelong was frightening. As a psychologist in private practice, I had very little exposure to individuals with schizophrenia. In the 1990s and the turn of the 21st century, most psychotic individuals were hospitalized for medication evaluation, then received follow-up outpatient psychiatric treatment and perhaps counseling or case management at a community mental health agency. Not many individuals with a psychotic diagnosis sought treatment with psychologists in private practice, most likely due to the expense of private insurance at the time.

After Jacob's confession that he thought he had schizophrenia, we engaged in what seemed like a whirlwind of therapeutic activity. Jacob received his official diagnosis and began a regimen of medication without inpatient treatment. Fortunately, he was able to remain at home. That was surprising, as I expected him to be hospitalized. Although often drowsy from medication side effects and frequent medication adjustments, he was back in school within a few weeks.

Of course, this was not the end of treatment. Normalcy took on new meaning and life became a constant challenge for Jacob. He experienced much disappointment and frustration. Many times, the obstacles seemed insurmountable. To this day, he still copes with auditory hallucinations when he is very stressed, and a lack of motivation and energy still can hamper his efforts to move forward. At the same time, who would have guessed that 20 years later he would be where he is today? Our story has not been an easy one, even though some of his achievements seem remarkable.

Why have I decided to write about such a personal journey that some would prefer to hide or cover up? My belief is that hearing the stories of how others cope with serious mental illness can offer hope, relief from self-blame, and encourage the healing process. A key element for troubled families such as ours is not feeling alone, but instead feeling that others understand and that finding solutions is possible.

Although there are similarities, the process of recovery from schizophrenia is different for everyone. Statistics may point to patterns such as the age at which symptoms may develop in predisposed individuals, or a medication's ability to reduce hallucinations or make thoughts more coherent, or the enhancement of treatment when the family is involved. Often people with schizophrenia turn to alcohol or drugs to self-medicate. For families, learning these facts and statistics is important in order to help their child muddle through the maze of treatments. There is a growing body of literature and specially trained clinicians to help with that process. It's just as important, however, to understand that the paths of discovery, treatment and recovery can be difficult and varied. A few may find complete remission of symptoms and some may live with long periods of resistance. Most, like Jacob, find ways to reduce and manage symptoms.

While being familiar with the statistics and patterns is vital, the academic understanding misses the human part of the sadness and the confusion associated with schizophrenia. Feeling alone, scared and confused makes the journey more difficult.

The goal of sharing our story is not to say that we have found the answer and the secret path to remission. I do know, however, that our family experienced some very normal emotional reactions on our journey with Jacob. Luckily, we found ways to survive and, more importantly, ways to help him. My hope is that our story will provide encouragement to others who are coping with schizophrenia in their family and that all who read this will gain a greater understanding and acceptance of the illness.

CHAPTER 1

WHAT IS SCHIZOPHRENIA?

According to the World Health Organization, schizophrenia is a serious mental illness that affects approximately 20 million people worldwide. While it is a genetic disorder, excessive stress is associated with onset.

Given that schizophrenia is so often misunderstood, I'm going to put on my psychologist hat for this first chapter and share with you the "official" definition of schizophrenia, according to the American Psychiatric Association's *Diagnostic and Statistical Manual of Mental Disorders V* (2013).

In this newest manual, the APA defines schizophrenia as a mental illness with the following characteristics:

Delusions – Delusions are belief systems that are not logical or do not fit with cultural experiences. An example of a delusion is when someone with schizophrenia believes that they are receiving special messages transmitted through their television or when they believe everyone on earth is an alien in disguise. Sometimes they may believe that they are a famous person from the past. Paranoid delusions center around others trying to poison, harm or plot against them for some reason.

Hallucinations – Hallucinations mean seeing, hearing, tasting, touching or smelling things that other people do not experience. Auditory hallucinations are most common and involve hearing voices that can either be internal (a voice from inside one's head) or external (a voice that seems to be someone outside of oneself). These voices can be commentaries on the person's behavior; the voices can sometimes talk to each other; and they can be commanding or depreciating as well. Other sensory-based hallucinations can include seeing things that others do not see, feeling touches when no one is there, or smelling or tasting something that no one else can.

Disorganized Speech – Disorganized speech is sometimes referred to as a formal thought disorder characterized by loose associations and tangential ramblings. In some cases, a person with a thought disorder may make up words or talk in incoherent ways that no one else can understand. Other times the thought disorder may be more of a reflection of the person's inner thought structure and may be expressed through confused writing or can impair verbal communication by being illogical, disorganized or rambling.

Disorganized or Catatonic Behavior – Disorganized behavior can be seen as agitated, excitable behavior, or even silliness. Difficulty following goals or performing daily activities is another example of disorganized behavior. Catatonia refers to lack of movement, mainly "woodenness" or posturing with an inability to talk or act in any way.

Negative Symptoms – Negative symptoms refer to behaviors of withdrawal such as lack of emotional expression, lack of energy, excessive sleeping, lack of interest in activities or social interactions.

Symptoms of schizophrenia are divided into two categories: positive and negative. The positive symptoms are behaviors that "add to" a person's experiences, whereas negative symptoms can be defined as behaviors which "subtract from" experiences. Hallucinations, delusions and speech disorganization are seen as increased stimulation and are therefore called positive symptoms. In contrast, negative symptoms reflect reduced stimulation and include low motivation, lack of emotional expression, inability to experience pleasure, social withdrawal, poverty of speech, low energy or drive, and inattention to social or cognitive clues. Not all symptoms are apparent in everyone diagnosed with schizophrenia. In addition, symptom expression varies among individuals in intensity and can change over time. Substance abuse can complicate treatment (American Psychiatric Association, 2013).

To be diagnosed with schizophrenia, a person must exhibit two of the symptoms listed above. At least one of the symptoms must be a positive symptom, such as delusions, hallucinations or disorganized speech. Symptoms must be continuous for six months and include one month of active or positive symptoms. Symptoms must also be interfering with daily activities. Other causes such as substance abuse or endocrine disorders must be ruled out.

At the time of his initial diagnosis, Jacob was actively experiencing auditory hallucinations – hearing voices in his head that he felt were coming from outside himself. According to Jacob, these voices began during his senior year of high school, around the time I found his "Schizophrenic Notebook" on the floor of his bedroom. His voices were very different from the ongoing self-talk that many of us engage in on a daily basis. These were loud, insistent or demanding, and very difficult for him to ignore by the time he was diagnosed. They interfered with his ability to communicate freely with family and friends, to pay attention to his schoolwork, and to find any sense of inner peace. They were not comforting, nor were they harmless. Auditory hallucinations impaired his ability to cope with life.

I recently heard someone talking about an encounter with an individual having active hallucinations who made light of the fact that the voices didn't seem to bother the individual and that they were happy to live in their "own world". There were existentialist psychologists during the 1960s and 70s that questioned the definition of reality and implied that maybe psychotic individuals just had another reality and that we should not judge their experience as right or wrong (Laing, 1967). (The prevalence and popularity of hallucinogens such as LSD during this time may have prompted some of this thinking.)

I do believe that people who are delusional should be respected or understood. Respecting others' belief systems is one of the positives that emerged from this existential movement. Acceptance and respect are important components of the healing process and important for human-to-human communication. Yet, I wonder, is it possible to exist in a world completely separate from others? Not easily.

What mother or father, for example, would want their child thinking that they lived on the planet Tralfamadore (Vonnegut Jr, 1969) or that everyone in the family had been taken over by alien inhabitants? Even if the voices or delusions are physically harmless, how can a person navigate the real world if they don't have some way to interface with the rest of that world? I am not talking about philosophical or religious or political sameness; I am talking about concrete definitions of reality, like "What is a traffic light?" or "Why do we bake bread?" If you can't connect with the reality of the world, you have to rely on someone who can. That was how so many psychotic people ended up in institutions before the advent of better antipsychotic medication. Unless you have one person who was centered in reality walking around with you every day, you most likely would not survive.

It was heartbreaking for me to see my son in such a state, questioning his reality. Jacob did not think he lived on another planet, but his thinking was disturbed. He misread social cues – a former strength – and he wasn't sure who he could trust or if he was saying the right thing. Hearing voices talking to him all the time and constantly telling him what to do was agitating and confusing. It was upsetting and bewildering for him if he tried to ignore the voices. Even the benign voices would become upset with him if he did not call friends whom he encountered in the halls at school by their first and last names. He said that he had to do what the voices told him to or he would feel totally off balance. "If I don't do or say what my mind tells me," he wrote in one of his journal entries, "I feel 'wired.'" In another entry, he went on to explain this conflict with his voices:

> I guess I don't have to speak or do anything when I am (truly) comfortable. (that my "voice" mind tells me to do.) (And as long as my head doesn't hurt when I "relax") "truly" might not (ever) come in this life (time).
> Revision: As long as my head does not hurt, I need not do or speak anything when I feel comfortable.

This is a reflection of the invisible turmoil interacting with others created for him. No wonder he began to withdraw socially!

I discovered this second journal, which he called his "Schizophrenic Companion", just a few years ago as I was digging through boxes in the basement. Reading these accounts revealed much torture and self-doubt. He spent much of the early phase of his illness struggling with what he called his "voice mind". One way to tame some of the dominance of this voice would be to only mouth words, which I never really noticed him doing. For example, he wrote, "If you 'have' to talk (if your mind 'tells' you to) and the situation calls for silence, 'mouth' the words. (but with no volume or sound)."

In another entry he described "If you ever get to (be relaxed to) the point where you know what a person's saying and/or going to say, 'mouth' the words (along with them), so as not to appear rude."

Reminders to himself appeared, such as, "(Try to) only use your 'voice mind' as a last resort."

He was worried that his voice mind pushed people away and wondered if it was a defense mechanism or a way to protect himself from getting close to others. "And/or it's situational/specific," he added. That seemed like decent psychological insight for someone feeling so confused.

The next entry attempted to clarify further:

I guess I should define "tainted": "Anywhere and/or anyone I use it (on)." ("It" being my "voice mind") Revision: "Anywhere and/or with any person I use my "voice mind" to get out of that situation (or to create a situation)

That defense evidently permeated our relationship as well. Although he never physically pushed me, according to his report, he evidently verbally pushed me away one morning before he left for school, although I honestly do not remember the incident.

Why'd I push mom away this morning? I'm starting to think she'll never know how much I care for her (because when I tried my "voice mind" on her this morning, I was starting to leave, I felt a growing emptiness each time I said what it told me to). But, then again, if I openly reject my "voice mind", that's like rejecting a part of myself and I want to have, no, need, to have complete unity and "oneness" with all the parts of my present physical body (and (sometimes) "being" if you want to go that far). I don't right now, since, with the "voice mind", I'm usually too impulsive to think things through.

How exhausting all that processing must have been for him!

Besides the auditory hallucinations, the other active symptom he displayed was thought disorder, which is exposed in his journaling. After finding his initial journal, I asked him to continue to write about his experiences when he could. As you can see, his writing was confusing and sometimes tangential or digressive. He did not talk in the fashion of a word salad, which is characterized by made-up words. He also did not do any thought blocking or sudden shutdowns when he was talking. All of these can be examples of a thought disorder too. Jacob's had more to do with his internal confusion that manifested when he tried to write. This confusion interfered with his ability to do schoolwork, mainly writing papers. His thoughts were very jumbled at first. He had difficulty completing most writing assignments. His early college essays reflected interesting ideas but he expressed them in an incoherent way. This eventually improved but he had to do many rewrites during his literature courses.

As a history major in college, he also had many written projects. He had astute, creative ideas, but he struggled with expressing them. Another quote from his journal said, "What I think and what I write are usually two different things... It's just one's more 'verbal' than the other." Eventually this symptom faded away and he was able to complete his coursework.

Jacob also had an overwhelming fear that he was losing his memory. He engaged in a flurry of picture-taking prior to his diagnosis. Evidently, he panicked that his mind was rapidly slipping. In a corner of his unkempt room, I uncovered a stack of pictures that he had taken in and around our house. These photos were of ordinary things that he was afraid he would not be able to recall someday – his car, our driveway, all of the rooms in our house, our back deck, me reading a book, our dog taking a nap, his stepfather's work bench, video games and his favorite souvenirs from various trips.

Around the same time, I also remember showing him how to make Annie's Macaroni & Cheese from a box so he would be able to find ways to feed himself when he became more independent in college. Instead of just watching me, he took pictures and wrote down everything that I said. Looking back, it now makes sense, but at the time his unusual behavior just seemed to be a quirky way to learn to cook.

This loss of his ability to remember ordinary things must have been immensely frightening to him. Losing one's memory is losing one's sense of self or identity. It would be like floating from one activity to another with no sense of connection, purpose or control. You could react, but with nothing in your past to help you figure out how to react. That horrible fear of losing himself could have easily led to hopelessness and suicide.

His early post-diagnosis journal also indicated this same fear of losing his memory. Referring to a recently played video game, he wrote, "Although I've written some of what happened in 'disc 2', I can't, for the life of me, remember what took place/happened during the rest of the game, and I can't remember the story, either. (or what it's about, in other words.)"

Frequently he entered reminders to himself, such as, "Ask Mom for those dates again," "Don't play video games during the week," or, "Ask Mom if I have any more of those wallet-sized pics."

Another was a reminder to "thank Mom for lunch again (for some reason she thought it was something special. I can feel a hint of it)." Some of the reminders were often centered around apologies or regrets, such as, "Apologize to Mom about the transparency that I didn't use for my 'TV Report'."

Many regrets peppered his journal. They seemed more in line with a critical voice that could lead to depression. Depression is a feature often exhibited by individuals with schizophrenia, especially in the beginning of the illness when suicide is a big risk. He wrote this entry in February 2001: "You have no idea how much it sucks to be a part of 'mainstream society' now; there seems to be absolutely no peace, or hope for peace at all; I miss the/my carefree days before the 'thing' and my 18th birthday." Then he added a quote from a song: "Oh well, soon you die..."

He mentions sorrow at giving away souvenir sweatshirts, trading a video game given as a gift, losing a watch he received for a birthday present, and even eating fudge cookies after his dental cleaning. He often criticized himself for being so impulsive, deleting video games when they didn't work as fast as he expected or doing something to the computer because he thought there was a virus. Later he would get very angry at himself for acting rashly. One entry included a long list of impulsive regrets: breaking a remote, not thanking people enough, unintentionally hurting others' feelings, buying things he didn't need, not keeping things that he really wanted, breaking a CD, etc. The list was long and his self-depreciation usually adamant. Reading these entries was painful for me, so I cannot imagine the agony that Jacob experienced.

These were the symptoms that his early medication attempted to diffuse. He did exhibit some catatonia (wooden posturing) but never long enough to make that part of a diagnostic feature. Catatonic episodes occurred pre-diagnosis and never lasted beyond a few hours. I describe these experiences in more detail in Chapter 2.

His negative symptoms included social withdrawal, low energy, lethargy and inattention, which intensified his already diagnosed attention disorder. These behaviors have been slower to improve. Negative symptoms appear to be the albatross of pharmaceutical research. For whatever reason, the positive symptoms have been easier to target. Many individuals with schizophrenia still have to live with negative symptoms even when the more active symptoms are in remission.

In the recent past, the schizophrenia diagnosis was subdivided into paranoid type, disorganized type and catatonic type, but these categories sometimes overlapped and became confusing during the treatment process. At the time of my son's onset in 2001, he was given the diagnosis of schizophrenia, disorganized type. He was not noticeably paranoid, but his thoughts had become confused and he was not acting like the carefree Jacob of his earlier years. The looming question was, of course, would his thoughts and behavior ever return to "normal"?

CHAPTER 2

A "NORMAL" START

Most people would say that Jacob seemed to have a typical childhood for someone growing up in the 1980s. To give you a little background, Jacob was born during his father's first year of medical school. I had already been a practicing psychologist for four years, but was only working part-time after we moved to Ohio for his father's schooling. I had difficulty birthing him naturally, so as a result he had an emergency C-section. He had some trouble with respiration and was transported to a larger hospital in Columbus, Ohio. His father traveled by ambulance with him, so he was never without family by his side. Before they left for Columbus, his breathing stabilized. To be safe, he spent the first two days in a NICU nursery anyway. Because he weighed 9lbs, 7oz, his father described him as the "King Kong" of the nursery! When he came back to the birthing hospital, I nursed him right away. We bonded well as I nursed him on demand, which was fairly frequently. I also took him everywhere with me in a front carrier and later in a backpack version. When he was very small, I even took him to a class that I was teaching at the university.

He met developmental milestones within an average range. He was healthy, inquisitive and loved to explore. Even as a toddler, he demonstrated an impish sense of humor. One time during a visit, his paternal grandmother was trying to correct him when he called a bird a duck. She would say over and over again, "No, that is a bird," and he would stubbornly repeat over and over again, "Duck." Finally, after what seemed like an eternity, she gave up and said, "Okay, it's a duck." At that point his eyes sparkled as he smilingly said, "Bird." This story shows not only the funny side to Jacob, but also his stubborn side, which has probably helped him as he faced his mental health challenges.

Jacob's sister Elizabeth was born three years later in Columbus, Ohio. Other than wanting to also wear diapers like his infant sister, Jacob adjusted well to having a sibling. I was working full-time, but was able to arrange a four-day work week. Having three full days home each week with a small baby and a three-year-old son gave me much more time to enjoy them. That year after Elizabeth was born was rather challenging, since their father was in Michigan completing an externship, though he would drive to Columbus to be with us when he could.

We moved several times during Jacob's first few years because of his father's schooling. We eventually moved to a Detroit suburb for one year, and another year, for a second time, to Columbus, Ohio, while his father completed his training. During those two years, I stayed home with the children. I have a lot of fun-filled memories of being an "at-home" mother. For one, Jacob's favorite food was and may still be peanut butter. He loved it so much that he told the neighborhood children in our Detroit suburb that that was his name. One time when he got lost at the grocery store, someone at the front desk announced, "There is a little boy named Peanut Butter who is looking for his mother!"

Another amusing memory occurred when we first moved back to Columbus. One day, our new neighbor angrily pounded on our back door with Jacob in tow. He had picked all of her ripe and not-so-ripe tomatoes and put them in his little red wagon. I am pretty certain he thought he was being helpful, but I don't think she called him Peanut Butter!

We finally settled in a suburb of Cincinnati just as he started kindergarten, and we lived in that house for 11 years. The neighborhood was supportive, the community had excellent schools, and the children and I made a number of good friends. When Jacob was seven, his father and I divorced. Although the break-up was not congenial, Jacob and his sister had consistent time with their father every Friday night and during the day on Saturday.

The kids and I still maintained a close relationship with their father's family. Their father's parents did an excellent job of staying neutral and joining in family activities with either their father or with me, but seldom with both together. His mother was always ready to help with babysitting, especially if the kids were sick and I had to work. She liked to visit us on all the holidays, but especially Halloween because she could talk them into giving her some of their chocolate candy! Their two paternal uncles and his cousins remained an important part of their life. Their father's youngest brother was Jacob's godfather and his other brother Jeff was Elizabeth's godfather.

Uncle Jeff traveled and moved around a lot with his work, and he met us at Disney World one year and we enjoyed exploring Epcot with him. Another year we visited him in Hawaii. That was an amazing vacation too. Jacob was about 13 and Elizabeth was 11. We hiked, tried sushi for the first time, enjoyed the beaches, and naturally went to a luau. We have very special memories of that time spent with their uncle.

As the primary residential parent, I focused on work and parenting but did not date for many years. The kids and I had a close family relationship. We spent a lot of time together, tried to eat meals together even during those busy activity-laden years, and we took many adventurous vacations. We also created many fun memories when we visited my family in Missouri once or twice a year.

During my single-parenting days, I introduced my children to camping. The first experience was more than memorable. We were on our way to Missouri to see my family and had planned to spend the night at a state park en route. We found a campsite just as the rain started. I did my best to show them how to build a campfire, but the rain kept putting it out, so we ended up eating cold beans out of a can. Then it was time to put up the tent, which was a small, older tent their dad and I had used years before we were married. After fumbling around for what seemed like hours, I finally figured out how to put it together. We then quickly huddled inside with our sleeping bags, trying to stay dry, our little toy poodle Amber curled up beside us. When the downpour hit, we realized the tent had not been waterproofed. All three of us stood up at once to get out as the tent collapsed on us. If anyone had been around to witness this, they would have seen three forms outlined by a wet, red tent and a yapping dog all scrambling to find where the door might be. We finally found the escape and spent the night in our van. Somehow in the future we had more successful experiences.

I did remarry when Jacob was a sophomore in high school and Elizabeth was in eighth grade. My husband and their stepdad, Glen, was worried that he would not be able to be part of the closeness that we had with each other, but he did an excellent job jumping into our circus. We continued to camp, travel abroad and spend time in Missouri. One of Glen's special contributions was the addition of three more young adult children. His kids were independent by the time we met, yet, at some point two of the three lived with us briefly. Our families seemed to blend well. Elizabeth was especially glad to have stepsisters, as she was the only girl in her father's blended family. Glen and his children introduced us to Indy car racing, and going to races became another early family connection for all of us. Before we were married, we rented a 15-seater passenger van to drive us all to Elkhart Lake, Wisconsin. We needed a large vehicle as his children had either a spouse or boyfriends to include. That was an especially fun trip.

Besides our blended family, Jacob's father remarried soon after our divorce. His wife had a small son, about three years old, and later they had two more sons. Most of the time Jacob was in elementary school and high school, his father lived on a farm about 15 minutes from our house. Jacob did have adjustment issues centering around the divorce, and saw a psychologist to help him cope with feelings of anger and confusion and his need to be assertive with both his father and myself. Jacob was very angry and often acted out this anger at both homes. He usually spent the first part of his Saturday nights with me in his room in time-out, trying to get control of his temper. He would lay on his waterbed and throw underwear and stuffed animals at his rotating ceiling fan. You can imagine how his room looked after about 10 minutes! His choice of release is humorous in retrospect, but at the time it was frustrating and sad. Despite how common divorce is now, it can be a struggle for many children who have little control over their changing family.

Jacob and his sister experienced the most conflict during the first six or so years post-divorce. Unfortunately for our peace of mind and my budget, their dad and I were in court on a regular basis. Finally, a breakthrough occurred when the courts granted Jacob and Elizabeth the ability to choose their visitation times. The change gave them more control over that part of their lives, even though they usually chose to maintain the same schedule that was originally established: Friday night and Saturday during the day with Dad. Tension and stress were greatly reduced as a result.

I saw many children in my practice dealing with similar situations of divorce and blended family adjustments. High levels of stress are not the cause of schizophrenia but can be associated with the onset later in life. I did my best to make sure that both of my children had support, good counseling and a consistent home life. Still, this stress may have had a negative influence (Stilo & Murray, 2019).

Overall, Jacob's early life gave very few clues that he would experience schizophrenia. Was he an angel with no issues growing up? I can't say that. He liked to challenge my authority. For example, he would practice his piano in the lower level of our house. What I did not realize – until his babysitter caught him in the act – was that he had memorized certain songs using his right hand to play the tune, while turning the pages of his comic book, which was in front of his music book, with his left. As with many kids even today, he loved video games too much, in my opinion. He had a lot of energy and was often hard to keep up with. One time when he was six or seven, we visited the National Zoo in Washington with my really good high school friend and her partner. They said that they had never covered the entire zoo in such a short time!

In fact, as a young boy, he was diagnosed with Attention Deficit Hyperactivity Disorder (ADHD). The ADHD diagnosis appeared to be an accurate one and is still descriptive of him. ADHD is genetic on my side of the family, and also could be related to birth trauma. He suffered a brief period of hypoxia (lack of oxygen) after his birth that was quickly resolved. He was diagnosed with ADHD by a psychiatrist at the children's hospital in Cincinnati before he was in preschool. His father and I decided not to give him medication in the early years. He was always full of energy, but his behavior wasn't a problem at home or school. I remember one time when he was three, I was interviewing a childcare provider in my home. Of course, she wanted to meet Jacob, and when I called for him, he excitedly ran down the stairs, slid across the coffee table in front of us, knocking everything over, and landed on his stomach on the floor. Needless to say, the woman did not take the job offer. I love to tell that story. Diagnosing him with ADHD did not require a rocket scientist!

We tried Ritalin when he was seven or eight, but he did not respond well. Either the medication or the dosage was not right for him. After school, he would have meltdowns, which I learned later can happen to some children. At the time, we opted out of the medication treatment. This was over 30 years ago; medical treatment for ADHD has improved greatly, and newer medications with fewer side effects have since been developed.

Jacob is smart and he did well in school without medication until junior school. He tried medication again in seventh grade and continued off and on during the early part of high school. When he took his prescriptions, his grades were more consistent. After the effects wore off, he required a lot of supervision to stay focused on schoolwork. Indeed, keeping him focused on schoolwork felt like my primary job as a parent. Sitting at the kitchen table next to him while he did his assignments seemed to work best when he was younger. Medication helped a little as he got older but he did not like taking it. Not long ago I questioned him again about his dislike of the ADHD medication. He explained that the medication made him "hyper-focused" and created a "buzz" in his head which he found "agitating" or irritating. Finally, in high school, he decided to only take it to prepare for major exams or when he was actually taking a test.

Jacob had many strengths. First of all, he was really cute. His smile and his twinkling eyes could be hard to resist. He was also clever and a quick learner. He was very social and could be really funny with his friends. Both my daughter and I remember how quickly Jacob made friends. Even on vacations, before we knew it he would be busily engaged in social activities with new found buddies. He took part in a lot of activities – Cub Scouts and later Boy Scouts, church activities, soccer, baseball, marching band and music lessons, specifically drum and piano. He liked to read and is still a very curious person. He enjoys exploring new topics, has a love of history and science, and stays up to date with national and international news. He also continues to maintain a large number of friendships.

Little did we know that during his senior year, Jacob would be diagnosed with a life-changing illness. In August, he posed for his senior photos. He looked handsome and ready to take on the world. He knew where he wanted to go to college. He knew that he wanted to continue to play in the band when he went to the University of Cincinnati. He knew that he wanted to major in history or biology. He did not date much, but he socialized with band friends. He and his sister were both in band his senior year and attended band camp together. His illness, plainly, caught us off-guard.

Could we have been tuned in to his diagnosis earlier? Probably not. Early or prodomal symptoms of schizophrenia often look like depression, teen angst or developmental adjustment problems. The diagnosis of schizophrenia seemed such a long shot that I would never have entertained it. Even with early warnings, Jacob was just his normal self in between the events that I am about to describe. He would quickly resume his very normal teenage behaviors and thinking. Even through possible warnings that may look blatant to others reading this story, the unusual experiences were short-lived.

CHAPTER 3

WHY DIDN'T I SEE THIS COMING?

The first odd experience that I can recall was when Jacob was about 13 or 14. He was calmly sitting on the couch in the family room late at night staring at the woods in the back of our house, fully dressed, and wearing his backpack. I asked him, "What in the world are you doing? Why aren't you in bed?" After more probing, he finally replied, "I am waiting for aliens to pick me up." Now that was definitely odd. As we talked, he didn't seem to be joking or simply trying to avoid bed. Since he played a lot of video games, I somehow rationalized that excessive game playing had stirred imaginative alien thoughts that were responsible for the experience. Still, it was rather bizarre. After that night, nothing like that ever happened again. I did discuss it with a neighbor, who agreed on the oddness but, like me, did not see other unusual behaviors after that either.

Perhaps another early warning sign was his reluctance to take his ADHD medication during junior high and high school. He had resumed medical treatment for ADHD in seventh grade but quit the medication by his sophomore year. Jacob did not like taking it. He thought he was not as funny at school and that it interfered socially for him. Looking back, the ADHD medication probably did interfere with his spontaneity. In preschool, his best friend called him "the joker", and that seemed like an apt description. Jacob always had a lot of fun-loving energy when he was younger. ADHD medication was most likely not as finely tuned then as it is today. Now the rule of thumb seems to be to take just enough medication to take the edge off hyperactivity and impulsivity in order to improve focus. Sometimes ADHD children do not like taking stimulant medication even if the dosage is low. In Jacob's case, he may have missed his joker self. But did it create or contribute to possible psychotic experiences or paranoia? Could it have contributed to the alien scenario? Treating individuals who may be predisposed to schizophrenia with stimulant medications is a controversial issue which will be addressed later. Some research points to a relationship between stimulant medication and schizophrenia if a child is genetically predisposed to schizophrenia. Since the event only occurred once and he did not take medication consistently, however, it is difficult to know for sure if it was a factor.

While in high school, Jacob continued to see his psychologist to cope with what appeared to be signs of depression. During that time, she administered the Minnesota Multiphasic Personality Inventory (MMPI). Even though I believed or hoped that his elevated schizophrenia scale reflected anxiety, which it can with adults, I did not entirely dismiss his psychologist's suggestion to have him evaluated by a psychiatrist. The psychiatrist diagnosed him with bipolar disorder, which at the time was the diagnosis "du jour" for teens with mood dysregulation. Neither Jacob's psychologist nor I believed it was the correct diagnosis, but we did agree that the anti-depressant that he prescribed might help with what appeared to be depression. The medication made him happy and silly for a while. It also eventually may have sedated him too much. Another real possibility is that his symptoms of depression and excessive sleepiness could have been early negative signs of schizophrenia.

That summer, when Jacob was 15, he exhibited another unusual reaction in a social setting. Glen and I had been dating for about six months, and since Glen had a tradition with his three children to go to at least one Indy car race every season, we decided to combine our families on an expedition. Two of his children brought spouses and another brought along her future husband, so we had a van full of young people joking and having fun. We stopped in Chicago for lunch, which was challenging in and of itself trying to find a place in downtown Chicago to park a 15-seater passenger van on a Friday afternoon. Somehow, however, after circling the same blocks over and over again, we found a rather expensive lot. At that point I readily agreed to pay the outrageous price because we were all so hungry. At lunch, Jacob was distant, often turning his head from side to side in an unusual manner. After ordering a large soda, he fell asleep leaning over his drink with the straw in his mouth. In my naivety at the time, I assumed his newly prescribed medication for depression and the stress of being around potential stepsiblings contributed to his behavior. I also thought that there was a possibility he was just attention-seeking.

Again, "normal" behavior would return for long stretches of time and these incidents would be pushed aside. When they did emerge, I found rational explanations that made sense at the time. In the autumn of his sophomore year, Jacob's grandfather Ed died suddenly of a heart attack. It was a major loss, as he and Ed, my stepfather who lived in Missouri, were very close. He had spent many summer vacations at the lake house in Laurie at the Lake of the Ozarks, and had shared many special moments with him in Ohio as well. "Grandpa" had been there since his birth, and was an important male figure in Jacob's life. You could say that he was the person who taught Jacob how to be a "man". On Easter Sunday, he showed him how to knot a tie. On the Fourth of July, he taught him how to safely shoot fireworks. On our many visits to the lake, his grandfather closely supervised him as he drove a pontoon boat, and he helped him learn how to catch and clean fish. He also gave him lessons about fixing things around the house and how to use tools. In other words, he was a very special person in Jacob's life.

I failed to notice how upset Jacob was until observing his behavior at the funeral, where he was one of the pallbearers. Looking at him sitting in the center of the church with the other pallbearers that day, it hit me how horrible the experience was for him. At age 15, he looked overwhelmed and could hardly perform what was expected of him at the time. On the drive back from Missouri to Ohio, he held Ed's army hat, special military pins, and a bullet belt from the Second

World War in his raised right hand for most of the ten- hour trip. These were special mementos that his grandmother had given him that weekend. He looked wooden and wounded. As we neared home around the Indiana–Ohio border, he relaxed and took on a more natural demeanor. That was the first time he exhibited a "wooden" or catatonic pose. It only lasted a few hours but the fact that it happened at all was disturbing to all of us that day on the drive back to Ohio.

At times during his sophomore year, Jacob would appear to be socially awkward. Like most parents of teenagers, I assumed that the angst of the teen years had struck. He really tried hard to develop friendships in marching band at the beginning of his first year at high school, and befriended two or three of the color guards who frequently offered to take him home. Even though he knew that I would have been glad to pick him up, he would start to walk to our house after band practice. We lived several miles away from school, so when these girls would see him on the road, they would always stop and offer him a ride. Pretty clever, I thought! It was certainly more fun to ride with them than Mom.

Later during his sophomore year, I did worry about depression. His energy levels decreased, he slept more than ever, he refused to take his ADHD medications, his grades suffered, and his social activities became more limited. His psychologist also agreed that he seemed more depressed. He engaged in regular psychotherapy with her and took an increased dose of the antidepressants prescribed by the psychiatrist. These interventions helped to some degree.

To make matters worse, around this time Jacob became a target of a hurtful rumor at school. In 1999, in the wake of the Columbine shootings in Colorado, high school students across the country were encouraged to report any unusual or strange behavior to teachers or school administrators in an attempt to prevent any possible recurrence of such a horrible massacre. Two girls that had befriended him in marching band earlier in the year became concerned about his behavior. Rather than being his usually congenial self, he was angry at another percussionist in his section that had been harassing him. At lunch he remarked that he really "hated" Jerry. Since the Columbine shootings had just occurred, these students thought it was best to report what they interpreted as threats to this other young man. In addition, they freaked out because Jacob had sent them Christmas cards and they thought he might be stalking them. While his anger at Jerry may have been out of character, sending Christmas cards to many of his band friends was consistent with his caring demeanor. Jacob was immediately suspended until his psychologist sanctioned his return. Even though she wrote a letter stating that he was not harmful to others or to himself and he returned to school the very next day, he struggled to overcome rumors that floated among some teachers and students. As a parent I agonized over whether I should send him to another school to start over or let him work it out. In the end, he wanted to stay and he continued to enjoy his band activities. He got through it and life went on.

The event, however, may have been related to some early signs of schizophrenic disconnect. Other friends and teachers said that he would wander in the cafeteria and stare out the window or walk down the hall in a wooden way. His behavior appeared eccentric. At that point, we decided to stop the ADHD medications, thinking that he was having a negative reaction to them. He didn't want to take them anyway, and Jacob appeared to be fine at school for the next two years with the psychological and psychiatric treatment that he received. I kept in touch with teachers and did not hear of any other unusual behaviors.

Looking back, it appeared that when he was under stress, he would withdraw or exhibit out-of-the-ordinary behavior. When he wasn't stressed, he kept pace at school, was active in band and church activities, and worked part-time at Kroger as a bagger. The pattern of withdrawing socially, however, was noticeable again prior to his junior year when we were on a summer mission trip with the youth from our church.

For several years we participated in a one-week Appalachian Service Project, usually in Kentucky or West Virginia. Many youth groups from different parts of the country would be assigned a week to help with a home construction project. That second year we built a deck for a family who lived in the hills of West Virginia. For at least two entire days out of five during that trip, Jacob slept like a rock in the back of our rented van. Neither Nick, the other chaperone, nor I could budge him, despite coaxing. In fact, Nick became quite angry with him and began yelling. His exasperation was understandable, as Jacob's behavior looked very willful. Eventually I made peace with his need for withdrawal and explained to the other organizer that Jacob was getting treatment for depression. Now, as I look back years later, I wonder if it was a misdiagnosis. Instead of depression, could these periods of withdrawal have been early signs of schizophrenia?

Later, in the middle of the same summer, Jacob ended up being transported to a hospital emergency room in Dayton on the last day of band camp. His high school would hold band camp for one week in July or August, and students had the opportunity to live in a college dorm at Wright State University. They would work hard learning their competition music and marching configurations in the hot sun all day and socialize with planned activities at night. It was always a fun time, capped by a performance at the end of the week for parents. That summer, I got a call from the band nurse several hours before the performance informing me that Jacob had been transported to the hospital. He had been carried off the field in a stretcher and taken by ambulance to the ER. He was alert, his eyes were open, but he was not responding. I left work, grabbed my daughter and headed for Dayton. I was given the wrong information about which hospital, so by the time I found him, he was ready to be released. The doctors could find no reason for his "alert coma" but for over an hour he was unresponsive to questions and unable to move. The nurse thought that perhaps his antidepressant dosage may have been too high but his prescribing doctor did not believe that was the case. It also wasn't a typical response to overheating – something that would occasionally occur at band camp. Whatever it was, he went back to camp and was able to perform with the band that evening for parents' night. Something had happened, but no one was able to figure it out at the time. The doctors ran tests but found nothing. Was this another experience of catatonia? No one ever diagnosed it as that. Catatonia can be a symptom of schizophrenia, but he had no other indicators of the condition at that time. Catatonia can also be related to other neurological disorders, but these experiences were short-lived and no one could account for them.

One other catatonic reaction occurred when my husband and I married at the beginning of Jacob's junior year in high school, the end of the same summer. He cared for Glen very much and Glen fit into our family well when we spent time together. It wasn't that he didn't want us to get married, but it was a huge adjustment. He may have been worried that my energy was already stretched by working and caring for him and his sister, so adding another family member might reduce my energy for him. It also might have been related to his father's contentious second marriage. Whatever the reason, the wedding must have caused him some inner turmoil that he had not really discussed with me. The day of our wedding, August 28th, was also a day that his high school marching band performed at the University of Cincinnati for a competition. The plan was for Jacob to go on the bus with the band, and we would drive separately to see him perform. After the performance, he would come home with us so we could finish getting ready for the wedding ceremony at our church. The band performance was outstanding as usual, and our extended family enjoyed seeing Jacob play percussion in the pit. When it was time to leave, he was not at the agreed meeting place. We looked everywhere but could not find him. Somehow, we eventually discovered him taking a nap on an empty school bus. How we found him, I will never know! When we finally made it to church, his posture was again wooden. His face looked like he was unhappy and uncomfortable. Viewing wedding pictures later, his poses were strange and emotionally detached.

After the wedding, one of his grandmothers told me that Jacob's wooden postures reminded her of her husband, his grandfather. She related that he had periods of catatonia following his return from battle during the Second World War. This should have been another red flag, but her explanation helped me to frame it as Jacob's reaction to excessive stress. I still did not consider that it could be a symptom of schizophrenia because I was not aware of his predisposition.

His grandfather did not exhibit symptoms of schizophrenia during the years that I knew him. For catatonia to be a symptom of schizophrenia, the behavior has to be ongoing for at least one week. For Jacob, these experiences happened and ended within just a couple of hours. The length of his grandfather's catatonia is unknown, but his grandmother believed his behavior was related to post-traumatic stress. I do not know more than that.

In between these possible warning signs was a high school boy who liked to learn and have fun. Again, periods of normality reigned as school started, Glen became stepdad, and Jacob learned how to use the trig calculator that Glen bought him for math class. Jacob and I excitedly prepared for the Thanksgiving break high school marching band trip that, overall, turned out to be a lot of fun. The band played in the Hollywood Christmas Parade and also performed at the Hollywood Bowl with other bands from around the country. I was one of the many chaperones for the 250-plus band members. We were divided into groups of two chaperones and approximately five or six students. Jacob was not in my group but with another very nice chaperone couple and friends. If you haven't been on a four- or five-hour trip on a commercial airplane filled with high school band members, then you don't know what fun really is! Earplugs and blindfolds might have been useful. In between performances in California, we visited Catalina Island, Six Flags and Hollywood, and some students went to the beach. Jacob and his friend Anna rented a golf cart on Catalina Island and had fun exploring the hills and vistas.

Something seemed amiss, though, during the afternoon that we went to Six Flags. I kept looking for Jacob, and thought that by the afternoon, he would surely be seeking me out for extra money. His chaperones reassured me several times that they had seen him, that they were certain all of their boys had gotten off the bus when we arrived. Other friends of his were pretty sure that they had seen him, but no one could tell me where he was. By the end of the day, I just knew he couldn't have been there. What teenager at an amusement park wouldn't want extra spending money from a parent? He hadn't made the request the whole day! I was definitely worried. With much help from administrators and trip organizers, we discovered that he had fallen asleep on the bus and hadn't woken up until the bus returned to the bus lot in another part of Los Angeles. He was waiting with bus personnel until they were ready to pick us up after dinner. Fortunately, the band director made sure that he arrived prior to dinner, and Jacob was able to eat and spend some time with friends. I have since questioned him about that experience, and he denies feeling scared or even angry. He said he still can't figure out why no one noticed him on the bus and woke him up. That is certainly something that I wonder about as well. I also do not know if that level of tiredness was a precursor to schizophrenia or evidence of a teenager who was really sleepy or wanted personal space. Most of us were exhausted by the busy schedule that we were keeping on the trip. Looking back now, his need for space could have been a precursory behavior.

On that same trip, he was sleeping during the scheduled time to tour Hollywood. In my "bulldozer mom" mode, I decided that he needed to be part of the experience, especially since he missed Six Flags. I kept pounding on his hotel door trying to wake him up. His roommates had already left. Because of his excessive sleep the day before and because he was being treated for depression at that time, I began to freak out. Why wasn't he answering the door? What if he had intentionally hurt himself? Finally, the hotel security guard opened his door and we found him huddled in his closet looking very fearful. My heart sank – I felt horrible. Thinking back, I still wish I had just let him sleep and have his space. Who knows what was going on inside his head? He looked frightened, but he told us that he was just really tired. He did finally get dressed and saw some of Hollywood on his own, and hopefully he retains the positive memories from this trip. Most likely he just needed space from being around so many people. Was that depression or something else? Looking back, it was probably the latter.

He seemed fine for the rest of his junior year, but behavior changes began to escalate during his senior year. In the autumn, his creative writing teacher requested a conference. Jacob's writing was very unusual, she said. For one, he would add lots of qualifying statements or asides in parentheses to his sentences, and she had mentioned to him several times that his writing would flow better if he did this less, but he continued anyway. I agreed with her that it was an odd style, but considering his longstanding enjoyment of *Mystery Science Theater 3000*, it seemed to be of that genre. For those who do not know *MST3K*; so, it will read, MST3K, the television program views old movies and documentaries, usually ones that are considered rather corny by present standards. An assortment of characters make fun of the movies by adding humorous comments. The show attracted cult viewers with an ironic sense of humor. Jacob loved the program and we spent some of our family nights watching and laughing hysterically. I had assumed that his new writing style was a reflection of the many asides the characters would make. Now I reinterpret the parentheses as a possible precursor to his auditory hallucinations. Perhaps his voices were telling him to add qualifying comments despite instructions from his teacher not to add them. This could also have been the beginnings of his thought disorder, expressed in his writing.

Then, two especially odd behaviors occurred the month or two prior to the discovery of his notebook and eventual diagnosis. One was at Christmas when my mother was flying from Missouri to Ohio to celebrate the holiday with us. The whole family, including Jacob, his sister, two stepsisters, stepbrother and my husband and I were planning to surprise her at the airport with "Welcome Grandma" signs. Jacob refused to get out of bed that day and I spent the morning yelling and harassing him to hurry up. Everyone else had left and it took a monumental effort on my part to get him going. I wish that I had left him alone, but I thought he was just being stubborn. My own stubbornness kicked in as well. He was an important part of the family and he should be there to greet his grandmother! It reminds me of a vacation when I was about ten years old that I took with my parents to see the Great Salt Lake. A nearby father had gathered his family in front of the lake and was yelling at them, "Smile, damn it! Look like you are having fun!" Well, we both eventually made it to the airport, but it was probably not worth the angry energy that I put into the event. Did that trigger his schizophrenia? Or was his withdrawal from family events a soon-to-be-identified symptom of schizophrenia? Of course, the latter is the most likely interpretation.

My guilt arises thinking of that morning when I so quickly jumped to the conclusion that he was being obstinate and purposefully antisocial. My yelling and screaming wouldn't have helped even if he were just being teenager-like, but it must have created much stress for him during those pre-diagnostic stages. Yelling out of frustration is an easy fallback for parents when we don't know what is happening or what else to do. Looking back, I wish I had been accepting and reassuring and had just let him sleep in. But how was I to know what he was truly experiencing?

The other odd behavior occurred soon after Christmas. Jacob was scheduled to audition for the marching band at the University of Cincinnati. As a percussionist, he had prepared his audition on the bells and drums weeks before the performance. When we arrived at the director's office, he had great difficulty making eye contact with him. Instead, his eyes kept moving from one side of the room to the other. I assumed that he was extremely nervous but his behavior looked psychotic to me at the time. He finally pulled himself together enough to tell us that he had not brought his music with him. As a result, he auditioned without music. He made the band and nothing more occurred until the notebook discovery.

As strange as some of these events may seem as I write them, they did not prepare me for what was to come. I don't think most parents would consider a diagnosis of a serious mental illness or schizophrenia when their son or daughter is coping with the challenges of being a teenager. The first go-to is usually teenage angst, perhaps depression – but not schizophrenia. It is true that most of the time schizophrenia emerges between the ages of 16 and 30, usually late teens for males. Certainly, then, Jacob was in the right age range for schizophrenia to develop. Unless, however, you have a first-degree relative – a mother or a father – with schizophrenia, that is not something many people would consider as a possibility. If we had known that he had a predisposition to schizophrenia, we would have identified those prodromal or pre-schizophrenic signs earlier. As we did not, the months following his diagnosis were filled with shock and fast-paced decisions.

With a referral from his psychologist, we quickly got him an appointment with a new psychiatrist, who was able to start him on the road to finding the right antipsychotic medication for him. The road seemed long and sometimes circuitous, but we eventually landed on Geodon, which helped him through his first few years of college.

CHAPTER 4

MOTHER'S GUILT

The first year after Jacob's diagnosis, it felt like we were caught up in a vicious tornado. At 18, Jacob faced finishing high school, deciding about college, figuring out how independent he could be at that time and, of course, making sense of how in the world all of this happened to him. At the time, it was as if our entire family was suffering from post-traumatic stress, and the world seemed ominous and threatening. Looking back, however, I like to think of it more as "post-traumatic growth".

During these early days, it was important for me as a mother and as a psychologist to first make sense of his diagnosis. Being a psychologist complicated my perspective of Jacob's illness. The biggest trap that I fell into was blaming myself or blaming the structure of our family. I kept wondering if I had done something wrong as a parent. Was I too strict or too lenient? Was I not available enough to him or was I too available and smothering? Or maybe if his father and I had never divorced or had a more congenial divorce this wouldn't have happened? Of course, if any of these parental behaviors caused schizophrenia, there would be a lot more people with this diagnosis.

In reality, if only I had gone to graduate school at a later time, much of this self-torture might have been avoided. So much more information has been discovered about the origins of schizophrenia and mental illness in general since my psychology training. During the late 70s, psychological theories identified the family as the source of schizophrenia or any serious mental illness. At first, various theories of psychology accused "schizophrenogenic mothers" of creating schizophrenia by being distant, unloving and unavailable to validate their child's experiences at a young age. Later, family or system theorists decided that schizophrenia developed because families sent double bind or inconsistent messages to children, thus confusing them. For instance, a father may repeatedly tell his son to never contradict him and then later make fun of him for not standing up to him "like a man." The belief was that children who were confused by parents' repeated contradictions and had no way to challenge them would adapt by abandoning reality. A psychoanalytic theory referred to as Object Relations Theory then purported that children who developed schizophrenia had missed an important developmental phase of early childhood that kept them from experiencing a sense of identity that comes from healthy attachments and predictability in their lives. If a child or adult with schizophrenia could be "re-parented" or find a way to feel like life was safe and consistent for them, then they would be "cured". Again, this idea was based on a mother's failure. Although these theories are out of date, they still persist to this day for some professionals and people in general.

Newer research has since identified serious mental illness as having biological roots with predictable stages of development. As a clinician I had read and practiced with the newer knowledge. Nevertheless, when illness struck my own family, blame and guilt took over. The what-ifs crowded out my professional reasoning. My earlier training flooded my brain with torturous accusations. I was convinced that I must have done something wrong. I spent countless hours re-reading old textbooks trying to find my mistakes.

I also researched newer internet articles about families and schizophrenia and interviewed colleagues, including psychoanalytic practitioners. The information was still confusing. Newer works were more in line with the biological model, but some also emphasized the role of stress. If families were stressful, symptoms would develop in predisposed individuals. Well, yes, Jacob had been under stress when his father and I divorced. But didn't he have appropriate counseling and support from his psychologist and his school counselor? Yes, junior high was stressful because Jacob did not get along with his stepmother and he experienced frequent conflict at his father's house. A change in custody and visitation that allowed Jacob more choices seemed to make a lot of difference for both Jacob and his sister. His stress and discomfort were not any higher than his sister's or other children with similar circumstances, but he was vulnerable. I kept thinking maybe I should have done more, yet at the same time, I knew more was not possible. Later I learned that these symptoms would most likely have unfolded no matter what circumstances surrounded him. Even though stress can be a precipitator, the reality is that no one can completely protect their child from stress. I was desperately looking for ways I could explain his illness in terms of my own contribution in order to feel that I had some sense of control.

I even made several trips out of town to consult with a psychoanalytic psychologist who was well-known for his work with schizophrenia. He had developed ways to help actively psychotic individuals feel more stable and in control so that life felt more predictable. His questions about Jacob's early development made me closely review my relationship with my son at an early age. Did he have transition objects? Yes, he was attached to two stuffed animals – "Kitty" and "Puppy" – which provided comfort to him in times of change. Such periods were always difficult for him but that is true of many children, as they usually like predictability. I did a pretty decent job of keeping his life regimented without being a fanatic about it. I took him almost everywhere with me during his first year. Front-facing and backpack baby carriers were popular during his early days, and I breastfed him on demand throughout his first year of life. Nothing in the psychoanalytic theory made any sense to me. I knew that we had bonded well and I was at least a good enough parent. Also knowing and counseling other families coping with schizophrenia made me question the poor parenting theory. In all of these cases, the parents seemed to have supportive relationships with their son or daughter.

Finally, I began to admit that these outdated psychological theories did not make any sense. Yes, some of the psychoanalytic methods may have worked as treatment. What individual with schizophrenia would not like to feel that their life was more stable and controllable? Learning ways to build consistency in a life that is falling apart can be helpful. Finding ways to reinforce a sense of identity and personal boundaries could help an individual reconnect with reality. The techniques and interventions that these psychologists and psychiatrists were using may have been helpful, but for different reasons. Understanding that treatments emphasizing consistency and personal boundaries worked, but knowing that the illness, not parents, contributed to internal chaos helped to take away my self-blame.

One of the journal entries that Jacob wrote before his thoughts became so confused said, "I'm writing in response to my declining physical and mental health. I am having trouble with day to day memories, so I will probably need to either write them down, make notes (hellooo schizophrenia), and possibly take pictures."

His notebook and random pictures of everyday, ordinary items were a reflection that he was losing his memory. He explained later that he was terrified that he would not be able to remember what his life was like, that he would lose his personal history and identity. Losing your memory is, in effect, losing your sense of self. How frightening that must have been. The worry and panic that he must have felt is hard to imagine. For this reason, it makes sense that, for individuals who may feel that their world is turning upside down, psychological interventions that provide consistency and self-boundaries could be useful. That does not necessarily mean that their previous life before a psychotic break was filled with inconsistencies, or that they missed an early phase of development that children need in order to feel secure. What it most likely means is that psychological interventions that help them feel some personal control over their inner experiences and sense of self could be comforting and healing.

Another area that worried me was Jacob's use of Ritalin and Adderall at different times in his life. I later began to read about the use of stimulant medications' possible connection to schizophrenia. Did stimulant medication contribute to his schizophrenia? Maybe – maybe not. The research is mixed. Some psychiatrists still prescribe ADHD medication for individuals with dual diagnoses, a psychotic diagnosis such as schizophrenia and ADHD. According to Pardini (2016), these individuals often benefit from the addition of ADHD medications and can focus and concentrate better. Some of my clients took both and did well with that combination. Other studies indicate that a serious side effect of taking ADHD medication can be auditory hallucinations, paranoia and impaired thought processes – in other words, they can contribute to psychotic symptoms in some vulnerable individuals. A later study in 2016 by MacKenzie and associates found that usage of stimulant medications is linked with short-term psychotic symptoms in children whose parents have depression and bipolar disorder, but not associated with children of parents with schizophrenia. Another study led by Huabing in 2014 found that individuals between the ages of 18 to 29 who abused stimulant medications and whose parents had schizophrenia were more likely to develop schizophrenia during a five-year follow-up. Neither of these recent studies implicate ADHD medications, or stimulants, in the creation of schizophrenia if used as prescribed by a medical professional. Still, physicians are now trained to make sure that they rule out a family history of schizophrenia or any mental illness before prescribing stimulant medications. Even if his early doctors had asked for this history, which I cannot recall, I would not have known at that time that he had any genetic predisposition. Jacob's psychiatrists since have been more cautious about treating his ADHD and have not prescribed medication for that diagnosis.

The what-ifs plagued me at every turn. What mother does not wish that she had a crystal ball to peer into the future and protect her children from every possible negative event that they might experience? In Jacob's case, I had to rid myself of the guilt of being a "schizophrenogenic mother" – a mother who missed his developmental needs for consistency and self-identity, who did not protect him from divorce stress, and who sought medical treatment for his ADHD without knowledge of his predisposition to schizophrenia. Somehow, I always brought it back to myself, and that way I could feel in control of a psychotic process that I most likely had no control over in the first place. Self-recrimination is so exhausting. Sometimes I think that motherhood is the birthplace of guilt.

Recent research into the factors that can lead to schizophrenia point more and more to organic or physiological changes that take place due to neurological pruning gone awry in the frontal lobe of the brain (Sekas et al., 2016). Certain genetic factors may contribute to this malfunction, which is why genetic studies indicate higher incidences of schizophrenia among close family members. I do not have symptoms nor does his biological father. Jacob does have a second cousin who was diagnosed and treated for either schizophrenia or schizo-affective disorder. Her diagnosis varied. She unfortunately died from a side effect of a medication that contributed to liver damage. Evidently Jacob has a familial connection which suggests predisposition. A common phrase used by the National Alliance on Mental Illness (NAMI) to describe the effect of genetic and/or environmental factors is the "roll of the dice". That may say it all. It means it isn't anyone's fault – it's just the way his genes unfolded.

Research published during the summer of 2016 may have uncovered the "roll of the dice" responsible for a schizophrenia diagnosis (Sekas et al., 2016). Earlier genome studies began to implicate genes as the culprit but were unable to identify which ones may be responsible. Now the C4 genes, which appear at levels 1.4 times higher in people with schizophrenia, have been found to influence genetic pruning during adolescence and early adulthood, the time when the condition usually develops. Excessive pruning in the prefrontal cortex, the front part of the brain, is linked to symptoms of schizophrenia. The good news is that research may be able to find ways to reduce the influence of the C4 gene prior to or during the pruning process. Because gene functioning is so interdependent, however, more than one gene is likely to be involved and separating the influence of each one can be very complex. Genome studies in general point to a complicated but hopeful direction in further understanding the neurological origins of schizophrenia. With enough research individuals with a predisposition to schizophrenia may not have to experience the severity of the illness or, perhaps, any symptoms at all. Wouldn't that be wonderful? The future looks brighter for generations to come, though that horizon is most likely quite a way off. Preventing the development of schizophrenia through genetic manipulation is fraught with difficulties and is not likely to happen anytime soon.

Finally, I began to realize that parents like me who blame themselves are probably looking for ways to manage a life that is skidding out of control. Letting go of my self-blame gave me much more energy to direct toward really helping Jacob, my family and myself. My fact-finding research lifted the guilt and allowed me to focus on helping my son move forward.

CHAPTER 5

FIRST-YEAR CHALLENGES

During this first year while I was in the process of searching for an understanding of how all of this happened, we had to face major decisions. Perhaps out of a desire for consistency, or due to my own denial that Jacob had such serious symptoms of schizophrenia, I stubbornly insisted that his life needed to go on despite his illness.

Looking back, I can describe myself as a bulldozer. I did everything possible to keep him on track with his peers. He missed very little high school despite his diagnosis; he traveled with us to Europe during his spring break; he walked for his graduation ceremony; he worked summer jobs before college; and he started college in the fall following his senior year in high school. None of these feats was easy or without challenges, but they happened. Jacob and I made them happen. Was I doing this for me, though, or for him? Looking back, this schedule most likely fit both of our needs. We were struggling to identify what he was capable of doing and neither of us wanted to give in to his symptoms.

It's possible that my persistent push for him to maintain this external schedule in his activities gave him a much-needed sense of internal consistency and expectation. Perhaps neither of us consciously understood this at the time, but it is likely that both Jacob and I were soothed and comforted by the structure of moving forward with life as planned as much as we possibly could. In retrospect, stability at this stage of his schizophrenia may have been a healing factor.

As mentioned earlier, he received psychological help and antipsychotic medication as soon as his symptoms were discovered. He did not have to be hospitalized so he stayed in his familiar home environment. He did miss some school initially as he was adjusting to his medication, but not more than a week or two. His counselors and teachers were notified via a conference about his illness and alerted that he may be fatigued in class due to medication. He also would need some accommodations to complete assignments in a timely manner. The process of finding the most helpful medication took many months. Most of them were so sedating that he would fall asleep in class. Fortunately, the majority of his teachers based his grades on the work that he had done previously. The school nurse later told me that if she had known about his diagnosis earlier, she could have arranged for him to remain home for the rest of the school year, and he still could have graduated with his class. She added that she was aware of several other students in the past who had been diagnosed with schizophrenia during their senior year. Accommodations were made to help them finish school at home. She also shared that these same students went on to college. That advice should have been encouraging and helpful, but I did not appreciate it at the time. The bottom line is that he attended school, participated as best he could, and was able to enjoy graduation with his classmates. He even had a large graduation party with friends and family, which he seemed to appreciate.

Prior to his diagnosis, our family had planned a trip to Europe for spring break. Since it was Jacob's senior year, we wanted to do something very special. All four of us — Jacob, Elizabeth, Glen and I — were excited and had spent many hours deciding what we wanted to do and see. When we were organizing this trip, we had no idea that Jacob would be diagnosed with schizophrenia in early February. By spring break in mid-March, Jacob's situation had changed immensely because of his illness. He was not a danger to himself or to others, but his psychiatrist thought we should cancel the trip. She said that she doubted that he would be able to remember anything of it. It is still hard for me to understand why I was so insistent that we travel anyway. Jacob said that he still wanted to go, and it was another one of those bulldozer moments that I would have during all of this adjustment.

Overall, the trip was amazing and fun. Jacob's medication was stable for the most part except he was tired much of the time. The medication also slowed down his cognitive processing, which stalled our trip at times. He took many pictures, which now help him recall places and events. I can remember being in Les Invalides, a military museum in Paris. Jacob has had a special interest in military history because of a class that he took in high school, and it eventually became his special interest as a history major in college. While the rest of us walked the many rooms and saw Napoleon's memorial, Jacob only made it through one. It was painful and sad for me to see him moving at such a slow, methodical pace. I couldn't help but think that this was the same person who, at age eight, completed the National Zoo in Washington in about one hour! His hyperactivity was certainly in check now. He appreciated what he saw in the museum but I regret that he missed so much.

Outside the museum, as we walked the Champs de Mars, we waited patiently – most of the time – as he carefully recorded photos immediately after taking them. Looking back, it was good that he could do that because he needed to have reminders later of all that he saw. At the time, however, the rest of us struggled to adjust to his pace. Traveling as a family always has those moments, but this did not seem like our usual process of getting attuned to each other's needs. During past trips, Jacob was usually ten yards ahead of us and we had to move fast to keep up with him. Quite a reversal!

This lack of "attunement" finally accumulated in an overnight train trip from Paris to Barcelona. I had studied in Barcelona one summer in college and I wanted to share memories with my children and husband. Elizabeth reminds me how exasperated she felt that night. We had reserved a sleeper car with four beds, two on the passenger seat level and two that folded down from above. She describes it as four people sitting in a closet facing each other with four large suitcases in between us. We had very little space, to say the least, and we had experienced a long day of sightseeing, after which we had to run to catch a train after dinner. Elizabeth had become extremely irritated with her brother, but cannot recall the exact reason. Most likely he was saying something to annoy us and he was probably doing it repeatedly. She is sure, looking back, that it had to do with his illness, because usually family irritations in the past were short-lived. In this situation we were all frazzled, exhausted from a busy day, and needed a break from each other. I suggested that we just go to bed, but the fact that we were in a "closet" made it easier said than done. The whole experience was like a Marx Brothers' movie. In order to change into sleep clothes, three of us would have to stand outside the sleeper compartment in a very narrow hallway with our over-sized suitcases so one person could find a way to open their suitcase and get their clothes changed in privacy. Since we each had to change clothes, that meant that this circus had to happen at least four times. After that, my husband folded down the top beds and, thanks to his engineering skills, found a place for the suitcases under and between the lower beds. Glen and Jacob took the lower bunks and Elizabeth and I climbed on top of the suitcases in the middle to sleep on the top. The beds were hard and we still felt cramped. On top of that, Glen snored most of the night and Jacob was grinding his teeth. (Either he was experiencing increased anxiety or teeth grinding was a possible side effect of his early medication.) Finally, Elizabeth and I both gave up pretending to sleep. We just decided to talk and enjoy looking out the window at the stars, the mountains and eventually the sunrise.

On that same trip, we also traveled to Provence. Jacob was able to see Pont du Gard, Palais de Papes and Le Baux-de-Provence with some of the ancient catapults and village ruins overlooking the beautiful hills of southern France. That was exciting for a future history major. Later we drove through the Alps into Switzerland.

During that leg of the excursion, Jacob excitedly bought a very nice Swiss Army knife as a souvenir. He spent quite a lot of money on it and did not want to part with it. He even slept with it under his pillow! I was still learning about his illness, and wasn't sure that was the best thing for someone newly diagnosed with schizophrenia to buy. At the same time, Jacob was the last person that you would expect to be violent to himself or to others. When we got to the airport to fly home, he had put the knife in his jacket pocket, forgetting that airport security personnel would abscond with it. Fortunately, we realized what he had done before we checked our bags and went through the security gates. Unfortunately, this was another time his cognitive disorder emerged. He was determined not to put it in his suitcase. He was sure that he would lose it and he did not want to part with it. No matter how much my husband and I tried to reason with him, we could not convince him to give it up and send it to Cincinnati in his luggage. Finally, we gave up. As we were checking our baggage at the ticket counter, he suddenly dashed to his suitcase and stuffed it inside. What a relief! Years later, Jacob explained that one of his voices had kept telling him not to check his knife, but then suddenly a new voice emerged that seemed to split away from the more negative one. This new voice said, "Put the knife in the suitcase or we will never be able to leave."

Even with the challenges, the whole trip was worth it to watch Jacob enjoying historical monuments and seeing parts of the world he had never experienced. Despite the few moments of stress related to his illness, we have many positive memories. But was it worth it to Jacob? Today, if you asked him, he would tell you it was. He often says how much he appreciated our European vacation. I asked him recently if he wished we had waited until he had recovered. He emphatically replied, "No. If we had waited, we would be taking my high school senior trip 16 or 17 years after graduation!"

He reminded me of many good memories and added that he also has many photos to help him recall our adventures. Sometimes Jacob says things just to be polite or nice, but his emphatic response to my question convinced me that we did the right thing to travel at that time.

When we returned home, he continued to meet with his psychiatrist and his psychologist. His medication was adjusted several times to figure out what would work best for him. Despite the fact that his symptoms were still not in control, he made it through the rest of his senior year, including a final band performance and his graduation ceremony.

Graduation was held at the Cintas Center at the University of Cincinnati. Family came from out of town to celebrate. When we arrived at the center, he was already dressed in his cap and gown. We left him downstairs to walk with the rest of his class as we climbed up the many steps in the bleachers to our seat. Somehow, I was sure that he would get lost or just sit somewhere in the building where no one would find him. I had convinced myself that he did not want to walk across the stage and get his diploma. My biggest worry was that he would leave the building and we would never be able to find him. My anxiety continued to skyrocket while I sat in the blue folding bleacher seat waiting for the graduates to march in to their assigned seats. Even after they came in, I continued to be uneasy. With 500-plus graduates sitting down below on the floor in folding chairs with red square caps covering their faces, it was impossible to tell which one was Jacob. When they finally called his name, I held my breath. Was he there? If not, where was he? Much to my joy and surprise, there he was walking across the stage, shaking hands with the principal and receiving his diploma. He achieved another major accomplishment despite his active schizophrenic symptoms.

After graduation, he still wanted to work a summer job as he had planned. He had been hired at Kings Island, an amusement park, prior to the onset of schizophrenia. He was able to complete his job training and tried several positions in different parts of the park, including arcade games, security and landscaping. One evening he worked late, which meant that he would not get home until around midnight. When he did not return by 1am, I began calling him on his phone without success. My husband and I continued to call him for more than an hour. By 2am, long after the park had closed, his stepfather and I drove to Kings Island and found his car in the parking lot. He was safely sleeping inside. He said that his medication had made him so tired that he did not have the energy to drive home. When he got to his car, he decided to rest his eyes and, of course, fell asleep. You can imagine how grateful we felt!

He finally gave up working at Kings Island. The hours were always variable, which made it hard to schedule medication at regular times. Also, he had difficulty finding a job position that fit for him at the time. He didn't feel comfortable collecting money or hawking games at the arcades. He didn't enjoy being a security guard either. Landscaping was too physically demanding because of his present energy levels. After leaving the amusement park, he tried busing and washing dishes at a nearby Italian restaurant. He lost that job because his supervisor complained that he had left some pans unwashed. After that he returned to Kroger, where he had worked during high school. Kroger was an accepting employer and the people there really liked Jacob. They always appreciated his friendliness and the fact that he was a hard worker. All in all, he was able to make some money, continue with his mental health treatment and try to find ways to cope with his schizophrenic symptoms.

By the end of the summer it was time to decide about college. He had been accepted in the College of Arts and Sciences at the University of Cincinnati. He planned to live in the dorm with a roommate and also play in the marching band like he had been doing in high school. Although he had struggled with his summer jobs and medication levels, his treatment was working much better by then. Nonetheless, going to college was a big leap. Even with all of my denial, I had to admit he may not be able to stay on track with peer-related expectations and plans for the fall. We used three events to judge whether he was ready or not.

The first event was the UC band camp held in August at a church campsite in Indiana for a week. This experience would be a major test of his social skills and how he would be able to live with others in tight quarters. The students stayed in large cabins. They would learn their music and practice marching during the day and have fun at night. All of this had the potential to increase his stress level, which in turn could exacerbate his symptoms. I worried most that he would shut down and spend the day sleeping in his cabin. Just sharing space with so many people, especially people that he didn't know, could have been overwhelming for him. Surprisingly, he managed it well. He had a good time making new friends, but he chose not to party with alcohol like many of the other college students. Fortunately, that has always been one of his good choices. Alcohol not only doesn't mix well with antipsychotic medications, but it can complicate symptoms of schizophrenia. He passed the first test by successfully finishing band camp.

The next event could have been even more of a dealbreaker. He and I attended the day-long orientation at the university. We signed up for the very last week that it was offered just to give him more time to recover and adjust to his medication levels. During orientation, he met with an advisor and got his class schedule while I learned about how to be a good parent of a college student. We touched base sometime during the middle of the afternoon. As he was walking towards me, he looked like his old self again. He was more animated and there was a smile spread across his face. He was so proud that he had passed some preliminary tests and was able to forgo entry-level math courses. His excitement about the classes that he had selected was contagious. Overall, he seemed to feel comfortable and at home on the campus. After that meet-up, I immediately called my husband from a bench outside the student union. "I know that you won't believe this," I told him, "but I really think that college is a 'go' this fall. Jacob seems to have the energy and the enthusiasm to make it work." He had passed the second test.

Thirdly, we met with advisors at the Student Disability office. That connection was a crucial part of his success throughout college and what finally convinced me that Jacob could go to college in the fall. He was given accommodations, including tutors as needed and a special place to take tests with extended time. He would also be able to get class notes from his instructors if he had trouble taking them himself. A support group was offered to students with disabilities as well. He made a wonderful connection with an advisor who was a history professor, as well as with two other supportive people in that office. It looked like college could really work for him. With trepidation, I agreed with his decision to start school in two weeks.

In summary, "success" during the first year of his diagnosis meant finding the right treatment and medication. He continued to meet with his psychologist weekly or bi-weekly to learn coping skills. He also met with his new psychiatrist regularly too. She continued to try different medications and dosages. After many trials and an additional consultation with another psychiatrist, at her request, she finally arrived at the prescripiton that helped him through the first half of college.

Success during that early phase also meant finding out what Jacob was capable of doing based on his progress and his personal determination. This stage of recovery did not mean that he was completely hallucination-free or that his thoughts were always well-organized. Learning to manage his stress was essential in order to keep his schizophrenic symptoms at a modest level. He was able to interact appropriately with others and he was alert and active enough to participate in classroom work. He knew where to find resources on campus if he needed help, and he was definitely committed to taking his medications and continuing with counseling.

He did not seem "too disabled" to move forward with his plans. With extra support, Jacob appeared to be capable of handling daily challenges of college life. Perhaps his determination and my own kept him on track with what he had planned to do following high school graduation. This determination may have provided therapeutic consistency in his life as well. In Jacob's case, this meant that when his world was falling apart, continuing along the path he had planned was comforting and reassuring. I encouraged him to keep going and Jacob met the challenge with similar strength and determination. Neither of us gave up, rolled over, and said, "Your life is ruined and you need to stay home and learn to knit."

CHAPTER 6

THE COLLEGE YEARS

Jacob started college in 2001 and completed his Bachelor of Arts in History in 2009. Because of his diagnosis, he qualified for assistance from the Bureau of Vocational Rehabilitation. With their help, Jacob was able to get tuition reimbursement and textbooks for his first four years of college. He had to keep his grades at a certain level, which he was able to do. Even though it took longer than four years to complete college, having those first four years covered was helpful. All I had to contribute during that time was room and board. This was a financial boost that made the eight-year stint possible without Jacob accruing loan debt. With so many other challenges facing him in the future, this was quite a gift.

Those eight years were marked by many highlights as well as some setbacks. While in college Jacob began to regain his social skills. His sensitivity towards others may have even increased. He opted for a random roommate assignment, and was paired with Nathan, a nice young man from another city in Ohio. They seemed to get along well enough. At the end of the first semester, Nathan decided to room with a friend he knew from high school. Jacob said the switch had nothing to do with his illness or behavior; Nathan had been feeling homesick and had wanted to live with someone from home. Jacob's next roommate was congenial as well. From the beginning, Jacob had decided not to talk about his schizophrenia unless someone asked him about his medications. He did not initiate the discussion because many people still had stigmas associated with mental illness.

Academically, he struggled with expressing himself clearly when writing papers during his freshman year. Despite his social improvements and his ability to manage himself on campus, his thought disorder continued to interfere with his ability to write clear, coherent essays in his English classes. Writing had been one of Jacob's strengths. He had even received a scholarship based on his score on the Ohio Achievement Test, which was taken prior to the onset of schizophrenia. Part of the requirements for a Bachelor of Arts was six to eight hours of English composition. Had we known that his writing skills would improve with time and medication, postponing those composition classes another year would have been much easier. Almost always his instructors would return the essays asking him to re-write his assignment in a more organized way. Jacob was able to get some help from tutors at school, though most of the time he would call me late at night complaining, "I don't have any idea what the instructor wants me to do!" Of course, the corrections had to be turned in the next morning! In my freak-out-rescue mode, I would drive the 45 minutes to campus at all hours. We would meet at the library, which must have been open all night. I would proof his work or help him correct his sentence structure. Did this actually help him? In the long run, Jacob probably would have done much better without my input. My presence likely just increased his anxiety. Looking back, I am sure that I was overreacting and being overprotective, but I so much wanted him to succeed. At least it is unlikely that Jacob ever felt abandoned by his family!

As a result of his incoherent writing and in spite of my late-night interventions, Jacob had to retake his English composition and literature classes more than once in order to pass that part of his core subjects. That seems minor in the big scheme of things, but it was frustrating to him at the time. His writing skills became an important benchmark to determine improvement in his thinking. Over the years that he was in school, his thought organization became clear again and his writing skills returned.

Early on in college, his reasoning and problem-solving skills were often compromised by his illness. More than once I remember falling into that trap of trying to reason with him without success. One time especially stands out for me. I can't remember the details of the disagreement, but it was related to a long-term school assignment. We had invited him home for dinner one Sunday. On our drive back to the university, we got into what seemed to me a ridiculous argument about when to complete the project so it could be turned in to the instructor on time. Both my husband and I were astonished that Jacob could even consider his plan because it was so irrational. I kept yelling, "Jacob, that is crazy thinking! That is your thought disorder getting in the way!" That was a horrible thing for me to say. Of course, he shut down. When we reached campus, we dropped him off without being close to a resolution. I will never forget looking at his face blankly staring back at me after he got out of the car. He had his own belief, and my approach completely bypassed his reality. As a result of that argument, I began to reconsider how we got lured into the idea that we could change his irrational thoughts.

Psychologist Frederick Frese, PhD (1991) helped people to understand how individuals with schizophrenia experience the world. He encouraged family members to listen to their loved one and make efforts to learn about their belief system, their thoughts, feelings and behaviors. While I personally may not have been able to change Jacob's belief systems that afternoon, just trying to understand him could have improved our communication. Like many well-intentioned parents, at times it was hard for me to avoid arguing with what appeared to be such obvious breaks with reality. How could he think such "crazy" thoughts? Why can't he just make sense? But, of course, such arguments were futile, if not counter-productive. Arguments about what was realistic and what wasn't just pushed Jacob away, which is the last thing I wanted to do.

Dr Frese and other mental health professionals know that reaching out to understand and accept someone's belief system, even if it doesn't make sense to you, is an important part of becoming and remaining connected. In this case, more respectful and diplomatic approaches to solving the disagreement might have worked better, especially if Jacob had at first felt that we understood what he was thinking. Expecting logical thinking doesn't go very far with someone in that stage of schizophrenia. Listening closely to what he was thinking and why he thought that way, rather than insisting that he listen to us, might have led him to be more open to other ideas or options. Certainly, if you are reading this book because you have a family member who has schizophrenia, you know that the journey has a steep learning curve.

Despite our occasional disagreements, Jacob would still call me every night at 7 o'clock. This was not anything that I had asked him to do. He came up with this idea of a regular daily phone call, perhaps as a way of making sure support was always there for him. Our conversations were not necessarily long. Sometimes I would be in a meeting and we would have to talk later. Also, he had activities that would occasionally interfere with the 7 o'clock time frame. Usually just a brief checking-in was all that happened. I can't say I objected in the least! It was such a welcome sound to hear his voice. I felt reassured to know that he was managing and was able to maintain a schedule. What a bonus if virtual phone calls on Zoom had been available! Having that face-to-face contact would have been even more reassuring to both of us.

Jacob's ability to find consistency in his daily activities at college provided much-needed reassurance to him. Calling me at 7pm each evening was part of the healing process. Going to class at a certain time, having built-in support on campus from the Disability Office staff, eating at regular times in the cafeteria – all of those routines provided external structure while he struggled with his wavering internal structure.

Consistency in his life was therapeutic, especially early in his illness. Creating anchors for stability illustrates what psychologists call object permanence. It is important when growing up or in times of extreme stress to know that you have an anchor or something that helps ground you in reality. For instance, during the recent COVID-19 pandemic, many people who locked down found comfort in scheduling activities at particular times, such as weekly Zoom meetings with friends, daily walks or exercise routines, or special television programs each evening. These routines are regular reminders that life goes on and that you have at least some control over or predictability in your life.

During the first three and a half years, Jacob found comfort in staying in the same dorm, even though he had different rooms and roommates. During his first or second year, his sister and her girlfriend visited him during sibling week. They had fun being together and experiencing the planned activities on campus. This may have been one of the reasons why Elizabeth decided to go to the same university after she graduated from high school. When Jacob was in his fourth year, she enrolled as a first-year student on campus, and she and her best friend from high school chose to live in the same dorm as he did. She had always felt a closeness to Jacob, and it was nice to be near a sibling.

Jacob met many of his college friends in his residence hall, in his classes, and also through programs at the Disability Office. One of these was a student support group. It met regularly, so he got to know other students with similar or different special needs. Jacob was very active in the group. He was treasurer for one year and vice president for another. Their goal was to be there for each other and to reduce the stigma related to having a disability. They decided to name the group DAJA, which stands for "Don't Assume, Just Ask", based, I am sure, on the many inaccurate presumptions that others make about disabled people. The group wanted to open up dialogue with other students when appropriate in order to dispel myths. He developed many good relationships there and is still in touch with his college friends either in person or through Facebook.

He dated several different young women in college and also had a group of friends who enjoyed making indie movies. One woman that he dated in college lived in Columbus. We had met Jill a couple times before, when Jacob brought her over for dinner. During the summer, we took him to Columbus so that they could see each other. Although Jacob drove in Cincinnati, my husband and I weren't comfortable with him driving two hours on a highway with which he wasn't familiar at that time. Evidently this young woman did not have a driver's license, so her parents did not act surprised that we dropped him off at their house. They lived near movie theaters and restaurants, so Jacob and Jill could find entertainment without a car. Like their daughter, her parents were gracious and friendly. The relationship with Jill did not appear very serious, but they enjoyed each other's company. She moved east after she completed college and she and Jacob remained in touch for a while.

He also enjoyed spending time with another young woman named Andrea who had schizophrenia that was more difficult to treat than Jacob's. She also finished college and later married, but it took her many more years to find a treatment regimen that worked. Andrea had to be hospitalized several times and took several breaks before getting through college. She was a lovely girl who was quiet and sweet and we enjoyed having her visit us. For her birthday, Jacob impressed her by making dinner for her at our house. He impressed us, too! We didn't know he could cook so well. She and Jacob are still friends on Facebook.

Another positive social experience for Jacob was living in a fraternity house on campus for two and half years, where he made some long-lasting friendships. His advisor at the Disability Office suggested it, and Jacob moved in during the middle of his fourth year of college. It was a Christian fraternity that would allow other male students to live in the house even if they were not official members. He met many nice people there and had an opportunity to be more independent. The fraternity had no cook, so each of the boys prepared their own meals. Jacob learned how to shop for his groceries and he figured out how to make basic "college survival" food. The atmosphere was supportive and provided positive social opportunities. He still maintains contact with some of those acquaintances.

The support that Jacob received from the individuals working in the Disability Office of the university was invaluable. Their interventions provided the structure and help that he needed to find his way through college. Someone always seemed to be available for him if he wanted to talk. In terms of academic support, as mentioned earlier, they provided copies of class notes if he needed them. He also had the opportunity to enroll for classes early to reduce the stress of finding the right class, and he could listen to soothing music while taking tests in a private space. The advisors at the disability office were especially outstanding. They mentored him, treated him with understanding and respect, and inspired him to do his best. As with his other college friends, he still keeps in touch with them.

Disability Offices in public colleges and universities can be wonderful resources. These offices follow Section 504 of the Rehabilitation Act of 1973. This federal civil rights law states that individuals with disabilities cannot be discriminated against in educational settings that receive federal funds either directly or indirectly. The accommodations can follow a child from preschool through higher education. This is different from Individualized Educational Plans for students with learning disabilities. Individuals with physical or mental disabilities may not necessarily have a learning disability, but mental disabilities like Jacob's impaired his ability to access educational opportunities. In my son's case, he qualified for various, useful resources that made it much easier for him to finish college. His needs would be assessed from time to time and accommodations would be based on what schizophrenic symptoms were getting in the way. He was able to adjust interventions as his needs changed. For instance, he had a lot of difficulty meeting the deadlines for his junior thesis. He was given a generous leeway to complete this requirement for his major. His stress was more manageable by the time he wrote his senior thesis.

During this early part of college, he met with psychiatrists and psychotherapists regularly. Jacob had a really good relationship with the psychologist that he saw in elementary school while he was adjusting to the divorce and intermittently during high school as he became more depressed. She is the professional who first diagnosed him with schizophrenia and helped him find good psychiatric intervention. He would take a bus to her office some 15 miles from campus because it was worth it to him. He remained in treatment with her for many years. Overall, she was a gift to Jacob and our family. Thanks to her, Jacob was never hospitalized and was able to meet many of his therapeutic and personal goals. She was an important support for Jacob until she retired some years later.

The first psychiatrist he worked with after his diagnosis helped him find Geodon, which for him was a big turnaround. After having tried at least three other medications, Geodon made it possible for him to go to college. It had just reemerged on the market with a new name after having some major side effects following its first launch. It was the only medication at the time that allowed him to function without sedating him while also controlling the voices, and he took it for several years with great success.

This doctor eventually moved to Chicago during his sophomore year. Before she left, she helped him find another psychiatrist closer to campus who specialized in schizophrenia. This one continued to prescribe Geodon because it was working so well. As with many psychiatrists, he expected Jacob to see a counselor in his office as well to help him manage the behavioral difficulties that medication could not address. Jacob still needed help with organizing his time, reducing the influence of his voices and staying focused on his schoolwork. Having two therapists, his psychologist and his counselor could have been a conflict for him, but he did not want to stop seeing his psychologist, so, he cut back the frequency to monthly. She was no longer on our insurance panel, so we had to pay privately. Even more importantly, traveling so far to her office every week took up a lot of Jacob's time. Staying in contact with her was still very important to him, however. As it turned out, the two therapists most likely discussed different issues with him, and he was comfortable with the additional support.

The new psychiatrist also added Lexapro to help with what appeared to be depression. He found that the amount of it that Jacob took needed to be adjusted depending on the time of year. In this early phase of his illness, I often went with Jacob for his psychiatric consults in order to be part of his treatment team. During one of these meetings, Jacob began verbally attacking me and being very rude. Every time I would say something, he would disagree in a verbally abusive and hurtful way. I don't mind it when he disagrees with me, but these were definitely mean comments. It was totally unlike him. Fortunately, the doctor observed this unusual interaction and believed it showed that Jacob was taking too much Lexapro, which was making him agitated. He reduced the dosage and Jacob returned to his more diplomatic self. He continued with this Geodon/ Lexapro combination for about a year and a half. This experience at the psychiatrist's office illustrates how useful it is to have having a family member as part of the therapeutic team. If the psychiatrist had only been seeing Jacob, he most likely would not have picked up on the impatience and agitation that Jacob was experiencing. Observing his interaction with a family member over time was a useful barometer.

After about three or four years, Geodon eventually caused some wooden behaviors, or catatonia, in Jacob. That can be a possible side effect from some antipsychotic medications. At that point, another pharmaceutical company had just introduced Abilify to the US market, and it became popular both as an antipsychotic and as a mood stabilizer. Jacob did well with this medication over the years. His voices would break through when he was stressed, but he could control them behaviorally by listening to music. Like Geodon, Abilify did not sedate him, and his doctors thought that it could also help him with his ADHD without adding any other medications.

To be clear, I am not advocating any particular pharmaceuticals. What I am trying to illustrate is that the path to finding the right medication for the treatment of schizophrenia can be long and varied for most individuals. Sometimes, when we thought that he was taking the "magic" combination, side effects developed and changes were needed. Like most people with schizophrenia, Jacob needed to be open to these adjustments in order to find what worked best for his symptoms at the time. Medication treatment varies greatly from one individual to another. I have sometimes seen clients in my practice who seldom make changes and have very little trouble with side effects. Others like Jacob will find the right prescription or "medication cocktail" that will last for several years and then need to be reevaluated. The good news is that the advent of newer medications continues to provide hope when the tried and true may no longer be effective.

Jacob really enjoyed those first four to five years of college. His confidence grew, he learned to manage his stress, and he coped with the voices when they became too distracting. Even with all of this progress, he still had difficulty completing graduation requirements in the traditional time frame. He had to retake his English composition courses and had to get extensions on writing assignments and essays in some of his history classes. He decided that he would be able to finish in six years instead of four. Considering the challenges he faced, that made sense and was not a problem. It was just gratifying to know that he functioned and managed his schizophrenia so well.

He had spent half of his fourth and all of his fifth year at the fraternity house. He had shared rooms with two different young men and found it helpful to have people around. He decided to live in the faith-based fraternity house in his sixth year as well. He had been included in some of their social activities and also enjoyed video-gaming with some of the residents. Because of seniority and because his goal during this last year was to write his senior thesis, he took an upstairs room by himself. This way he could have more privacy.

Like many college students getting ready to graduate, having a room to himself seemed like prime real estate at the time. What was supposed to be a prized arrangement, however, proved to be a disaster. He had no idea that, for him, having that much solitude and quiet would lead to a second episode of overwhelming auditory hallucinations and distorted thinking. He attributes his second flare-up to being "too alone". He had become very comfortable with the friends he had made at the fraternity and didn't realize how much their presence had helped him.

I remember receiving the call from the president at the fraternity house: "Jacob has locked himself in his room for over a week. He has not gone to class nor even gone down to the kitchen to eat. We can't get him to open his door." When I arrived and finally convinced him to let me in, I couldn't believe what I saw. His room was a total mess, with trash, books and clothes strewn from one wall to the other.

Boxes that he had used to move upstairs were upended, his belongings falling onto a floor inches deep with clutter. Jacob was curled up on his mattress with no sheet, afraid to leave his space.

More recently we have talked about what triggered this setback. He explained that having roommates and friends nearby are mental anchors for him. He likes to know that someone is around in case he needs a check on his thinking. He describes being alone as giving his disorder a field day. He believes that when his room became messy and chaotic, his mind "just went crazy". He added that quietness makes sense for "normal" people, but not for him. This revelation provides useful insight and explains why relationships with others can be comforting and calming for him. Interacting with others provides distraction from the voices, reassurance that life continues to go on around him, and perhaps a sense of structure in order to organize himself and his space.

We immediately packed his belongings and moved him home. He withdrew from classes that semester. He wasn't able to focus on coursework, let alone research and write his thesis. Also, he was in no shape to drive the 45-minute commute from our house to the university and back. Continuing to go to school was simply not an option. Instead, we set about getting more intensive psychiatric and psychological help to work through his setback. During this time, he was not sleeping and was acting very agitated. Because it was a weekend and it seemed like something needed to be done right away, we took him to the ER at Good Samaritan Hospital. The psychiatrist on duty gave him medication and released him. I thought for sure that he would be admitted to an inpatient unit. Even then he still did not qualify for hospitalization because he was not harmful to himself or others.

Being at home in his own room provided some comfort. He had his own bed, home-cooked meals and interactions with Glen and with me when we were home. He needed more structure and more heightened therapy, though, so he participated in an outpatient program at a nearby hospital in our county. By the time he started the program, he was able to drive himself. The program began at nine and ended around two or three in the afternoon. During that time, he received psychiatric consultations with a new psychiatrist, who added Trileptal to help reduce anxiety. He also benefited from individual psychotherapy, group therapy and instructions on daily living skills to help him organize his time. He was able to gain a sense of direction following the three-week program. He eventually found employment working in retail at a computer store. By the end of the semester, he had returned to his former level of functioning. He was again able to control his stress levels, including the intrusive auditory hallucinations. His thoughts were more organized and his social interests were more solid. He decided to try to take one class during the spring semester. Since that was successful, he began to add a few more classes in the summer and the following year. He never returned to full-time status, but he was near the end of his coursework anyway.

During this time, we decided to pursue his psychiatrist's suggestion of getting government disability assistance. I had resisted this suggestion until Jacob's relapse. The doctor had explained that Supplemental Security Income (SSI) or Social Security Disability Income (SSDI) could be a good option. Having done evaluations for the state of Ohio for people applying for disability, I knew that both benefits are managed by Social Security. SSI is designed for adults and children who have never worked or who have not accumulated enough work credits and have limited financial resources. In contrast, SSDI provides income based on credits earned working at jobs that have Social Security. To qualify for either benefit, Jacob had to prove that a physical or mental health diagnosis interfered with his ability to work. Since we were not sure of the full range of his abilities to work and support himself in the future, we thought it would be helpful for him to have some income to rely on. Also, by qualifying for a state disability, he would be able to receive a case manager and other community treatment benefits including Medicare.

What we quickly discovered was that applying for Social Security Disability can be a convoluted maze of forms and hearings. I initiated an internet application, which was quite detailed, and then we waited for a response. Evidently, the length of time varies based on how many applicants the state receives at the time. It is possible to also hire an attorney who specializes in the disability application process. They are often willing to help for a portion of the fee received from the government if the request is accepted. Another less costly resource is a case manager at the county community behavior health agency. From what I understand, neither of these resources would necessarily speed up the response time. As is usually the case, we experienced denials and delays once the application was submitted. I have known of clients who were able to sweep right through the process on the first try, but that is not very common. We waited many months before we heard from the disability office that Jacob had been rejected. Because the application was rather daunting, this news was especially disappointing. We appealed the decision, but felt less hopeful than we had felt initially.

During the appeal process, Jacob met with a state disability evaluator. Because schizophrenia can sometimes be an invisible disability, it is probably helpful for the evaluator to interview a family member or the treating doctors, too. In my son's case, Jacob did not seem to have problems getting employment, but, during his early years, he did have difficulty maintaining jobs. He would not actually get fired for behavior relating to his schizophrenia, but he usually stopped going to work, which led to losing his job. To a disability evaluator, this can look like willful lack of motivation. To someone who understands serious mental illness, it looks symptomatic and typical – perhaps due to difficulty with follow-through, the negative schizophrenic symptom of apathy and lethargy, and/or difficulties with stress management. Jacob usually managed stress early on – and still can – by sleeping and playing video games. Identifying and talking about stress was hard for him at that time. On many occasions in the past, he did not have the insight that he has now about his symptoms, or he may have just had difficulty describing his experiences to the evaluator. His lack of insight and difficulty with communication may have contributed to his second rejection. The evaluator had asked, "Do you think that you are capable of working?", and Jacob responded by saying, "Yes," adding that he thought he didn't really need disability help. That answer, plus his pattern of work inconsistency, must have led the evaluator to believe that he was just being lazy. Having an attorney or a case manager that understood his illness might have changed the direction of the application.

We finally did find an attorney who could help us and were scheduled to have another hearing with the state when, voila – Jacob got another job! On the attorney's advice, we dropped the application but held on to all of the paperwork in case we needed it in the future, as we were not sure if this pattern of fading away would occur again. In the end, Jacob kept this job for about two years until he finished college and wanted to find other employment. Even after all of this time, I still can't bring myself to toss out the two-inch-thick application, which remains in my file cabinet to this day.

Having Jacob home again felt safe, but it did not always mean smooth sailing. In fact, I was not sure if the plan to live at home and commute to school was going to work. He often procrastinated by playing lots of video games, and he slept a lot, probably as an avoidance strategy or maybe due to the negative symptoms of schizophrenia. I knew his classes would be demanding, but I was able to see first-hand how he dealt with stress, which was to avoid doing anything productive. I found myself constantly nagging him to get busy with his schoolwork and then second-guessing myself about how much I might be adding to his stress. Was my harassment what was really needed for him to finally finish? It seemed that he relied on me for motivation, almost as if I had become one of his voices. That was an exhausting time for both of us.

I did feel a sense of relief having him at home and being able to monitor the progress of his mental health. He began to reach out to friends at the university again and even invited some of them to the house. We enjoyed meeting his college acquaintances. Eventually he began to date a young woman named Sally who was part of his social group at school. Dating Sally revealed to us how his social discernment skills had been diminished during this phase of his illness.

Jacob was a social, outgoing young man with a great sense of humor and a lot of energy prior to the onset of his schizophrenia symptoms. During the early years of his illness, he lost some of his social judgment and became vulnerable to people that did not have good intentions. He would often misunderstand social cues. Throughout this time, however, he continued to be kind, caring and concerned about others. On the one hand, these traits made him a nice person to be around; on the other, they made him very vulnerable.

That being said, initially Sally pursued Jacob. He debated about how serious he wanted to make their friendship and finally decided to date her outside the group. Sally turned out to be controlling, mean and at times physically aggressive. Jacob's vulnerability led him to accepting her outbursts and perhaps feeling responsible for her anger, which is a typical response pattern of someone who is in an abusive relationship. His vulnerability is also typical of someone with schizophrenia. People with this condition are much more often victims of violence rather than perpetrators. (I will elaborate more on this later.) He told me more recently that he had felt traumatized and fearful of her most of the time they dated. One evening he had fallen asleep on the couch at her parent's house. She approached him with a pillow and tried to smother him. According to him, her mother walked in on the scene in the nick of time, which he believes saved him. Somehow, he eventually escaped that relationship, but it was hard for him to let go of his attachment to her nonetheless. As with most victims of domestic violence, he had trouble both exiting the relationship and trusting his next, more positive partner.

Part of his difficulty letting go of the relationship with Sally may have been his commitment to consistency. He did not like changes. He preferred structure and the comfort that comes with the familiar, even if it is not always in his best interest. In addition, his self-esteem may have been negatively impacted by his schizophrenia. He may have believed that he would not be able to find a better relationship because of his illness and he did not want to be alone. Jacob has said that being by himself was perhaps his biggest fear that kept him in the relationship. Even to this day he prefers to have people around. Fortunately, his relationships are healthier now.

The good news is that despite this abusive dynamic with Sally, Jacob did not give up on relationships. Soon after this one ended, he began interacting on Facebook with a young woman who lived in a nearby community. She was about eight years younger than he was, but they seemed to have much in common. They met in person one night at a coffee shop in a local bookstore, talked until the bookstore closed, and then came to our house so he could introduce her to us and continue to talk. It was a marathon first date. She was very different from Sally. Rachel was much kinder, had a good sense of humor, and was definitely more supportive. He continued to date her while he was finishing his last classes and his senior history thesis.

Did his relationship with Sally leave any scars? Most likely it contributed to a lot of communication difficulties with Rachel in the beginning of their relationship. His paranoia interfered with trusting her when they were not together and made it difficult to focus at work and on school projects. Although he never really met the criteria for paranoia as described in the definition of someone with paranoid schizophrenia, he definitely had trust issues. This may have been more related to low self-esteem rather than actually believing that Rachel was plotting against him. In addition, the paranoia was relatively time-limited. Now it no longer seems to get in the way of his relationship or his work, perhaps due to good therapy and because his trust in Rachel continued to improve as the relationship matured. New relationships often have baggage to face, and his baggage was heavy.

Rachel knew from the beginning that Jacob coped with symptoms of schizophrenia. She had exposure to mental illness in her family while growing up, so entered the relationship with open eyes. At the same time, he functioned quite well with his medications, and his symptoms were not easily observed by others. At this point, he exhibited no issues related to his illness that interfered with their relationship other than the initial distrust. This phase was characterized by hope and optimism, much like any new relationship.

Both were working retail jobs, Jacob was finishing his degree, and she, at 18, hoped to go to college at a later time. She was living at home and so was Jacob.

Just as he was finishing his last class and his senior thesis, his father offered to let him live in a farmhouse that he owned. The empty property had several bedrooms, which his father had planned to lease to other tenants at the same time. This would have involved sharing space with people Jacob did not know and who may not have needed quiet space to finish college. Since his relapse, he had been living with his stepfather and me. He had the privacy and structure in our home that he needed to concentrate on his classes and senior project. His computer and schoolbooks were in the corner of his rather large bedroom upstairs, while his stepfather and I spent much of our time downstairs. It was familiar space for him, since he had lived in this house while he was in high school. It afforded consistency, which has been important for him. The offer from his father would have been perfect if he had already finished college and did not need the structure of home to get through it. Unfortunately, Jacob was in a difficult position. He was caught between Dad's encouragement to move into the farmhouse and Mom's push for him to stay in his present situation until he graduated. The episode created a lot of misunderstanding between Jacob and me, and probably between him and his father, too. In the end, his need for consistency prevailed for a few more months. He stayed at our home until he graduated, and then moved out to live with Rachel, who soon became his wife.

CHAPTER 7

POST-COLLEGE STRUGGLES

Jacob had met some pretty remarkable goals during the past eight years. For one, he graduated from college with a bachelor's degree in history in June 2009 – no small feat considering his active symptoms of schizophrenia at the beginning and a relapse in the middle of his program. I am sure that he felt very proud of this accomplishment, as did we all. The road was bumpy and difficult, but Jacob worked hard and persevered.

Secondly, he had a full-time job. Granted, working at Kroger may not have been his dream job, but it was steady and provided good enough pay. Thirdly, he was living independently with his future wife. He and Rachel rented a condo from her aunt in Cincinnati for a while, which gave them privacy, some independence, and a great view of the city. His confidence was growing more and more, and it was heartwarming to see him so happy.

Life should have been easier now, right? Unfortunately, there were still downsides.

For one, Jacob may have had social independence, but his financial independence still came up short. His finances were complicated not just by his disability, but by the 2008 economic recession. With a degree in history, he had not planned to still be working at Kroger. Jacob's financial struggles were shared by many in his age group. Actually, I saw a fair amount of that dynamic in my practice. During that time, new college graduates would seek short-term therapy to try to find ways to cope with the slow job market and living at home after being so independent in college. In addition, Jacob still needed our insurance to cover medical expenses. Fortunately, because of his disability, our family policy allowed him to be a dependent until he married. At the end of each month, he and Rachel often ran short of money for daily living expenses. Thinking and hoping his financial situation was temporary, my husband and I would sometimes bail them out. He always seemed to be just a heartbeat away from full independence.

Did his diagnosis make him a slacker? Absolutely not! Jacob was a hard worker. His supervisors and co-workers viewed him as a conscientious employee, a fast learner and a nice person. Prior to graduation, he was hired by Comp USA. He worked in retail sales at first and was later promoted to merchandiser. They recognized his enthusiasm and his computer knowledge. More promotions were most likely on the horizon. Unfortunately, Comp USA was a victim of the recession and within a year the store closed. What looked like a possible career path was no longer available to Jacob.

His Kroger experience did not end well, either. His supervisor in the deli appreciated his work and was disappointed when Jacob found a computer-related job that he really wanted. As a way to help him and keep her department staffed, she offered him part-time hours and insurance benefits for a while. The arrangement was enticing, since he would be on probation at the new company and would not have benefits at first. Unfortunately, the plan did not work out well for anyone. Working two jobs became too stressful and he just couldn't keep up. Instead of discussing the situation with her, he stopped showing up for work. He fell back on his pattern of fading away rather than being assertive with his supervisor and telling her that he didn't want to work two jobs. Looking back, he probably regrets that decision now. Even if the job itself was not his dream position, he liked and respected the supervisor. Also, having her as a reference would have been nice too. The good part, however, was that he now had to push himself into new areas of employment rather than relying on his safe fallback. Having worked at Kroger off and on since he was 14, whenever he really needed to work, he could count on finding a job there. Now the option was off the table.

So, with a degree in history, why wasn't he using the skills he learned in school? When he first graduated from college, he did want to find a job that fit his academic background and interests. Finding one, however, was not so easy. He did not want to teach, as he thought a classroom filled with students would be too stressful and that organizing lessons would have been difficult for him. Graduate school was a possibility, but he did not feel ready for more studies. Museum jobs were scarce in his area, and what positions were available did not interest him.

He also tried retail sales for a while, but the pay was not that rewarding. He applied for some supervisory positions and after interviewing for a few management tracks, he decided that he would feel too much pressure in those roles. Besides being unsure whether he had the required organizational skills, he would be expected to cope with unhappy employees or disgruntled customers. Jacob may have been too mild-mannered for those kinds of confrontations.

Finally, one day he called me very excitedly, saying, "I have decided that I really want to work in the field of computers! I have found a great place to get training. Will you come to the admissions meeting with me?" We were both impressed during the interview. The institution offered various training programs. He chose the technical support path. The school provided in-person classes followed by independent lab work. In the end, he could test for certifications that would qualify him for computer support employment.

A word to the wise: never underestimate the usefulness of academic accommodations! Looking back, we should have requested a 504-disability accommodation plan like he had in high school and college. At this point we both just assumed that he could do the training without special interventions. Also, by that time, I was concerned about stigma in the workplace. What if his diagnosis of schizophrenia prevented him from finding a job? In the end, Jacob could not keep up with the pace of the program. Concentrating in the classroom was difficult. The work took longer for him because many students used the computer labs – their presence was a distraction. Intellectually, he was more than capable of grasping the material, but he needed to work at his own pace with more privacy. The entire endeavour turned out to be a major waste of money and a setback to Jacob's self-confidence.

The takeaway from the whole experience was that Jacob learned that he could do better with self-study. Eventually he found a career path in the field of computer support that he really liked and that fit for him. He purchased study materials for several certifications, prepared at home with fewer distractions, and he passed every exam that he took. The best part was that he began to find contract employment that he really enjoyed.

Unforeseen complications arose, however. Contract technology jobs meant that he would work for a specified period of time at a site. When that project was complete, he would then be transferred to another site. Sometimes there were unpaid gaps between assignments. Initially at his work sites, he was able to maintain a decent pace during training and in the early weeks that followed. If expectations increased or changed, Jacob struggled to keep up with the pace or adjust to new demands. For instance, one help desk role morphed into a sales position. Telephone work created too much anxiety for him. He was seldom fired, but he got into a habit of quitting before finding a replacement job. The pressure would accumulate to such a degree that he would either resign on the spot or stay home and sleep.

Was I frustrated? Of course – I was at my wit's end! As this pattern continued, I realized that I could not continue to provide the additional financial support that was needed to keep him in his apartment. Few options were available. Subsidized housing was off the table due to the economic problems in the country. Government housing programs were not even offering a waiting list. Jacob did not want to apply for disability again. Consequently, my husband and I invited Jacob and Rachel to live with us until they could figure out what they wanted to do. That offer appeared to be the turning point, another leap of progress towards figuring out what they had to do to be independent. They realized that they did not want to live with us and give up their autonomy. As a result, they never moved in. I am sure moving back to Mom's would have felt like a step back, so they somehow found a way to get by. They relocated to an apartment that they could afford and must have cut back on expenses.

They found an apartment in a community about 15 minutes north of where my husband and I lived. It had two bedrooms with a nice balcony and a pool. Eventually Rachel's older brother Terry moved in with them, which gave them some additional income. The arrangement was a help to Terry too. He had been living with his grandmother, but she became too ill to live independently, so had moved in with one of her sons. Because Terry's mobility was limited by cerebral palsy, he needed to live where he could get help. Rachel could grocery shop and run errands for him and Terry became a video game companion for Jacob and a friend who agreed with his political views. The arrangement was a win-win for all.

Terry was Rachel's brother from her mother's previous marriage. Their mother was deceased and both had been living with their maternal grandmother when Rachel and Jacob met. Terry receives government assistance because he is unable to work, and for the most part, he prefers to stay in his room. Besides Jacob and Rachel, his main connection to the world is his computer. He appears to be very bright and stays current on political affairs. Jacob enjoys his company and their many conversations.

The biggest surprise, however, was yet to come. During all this moving and adjusting, Jacob and Rachel caught all of us off guard by getting married. Yes, they had been engaged. In fact, they were planning a family wedding at his father's country club for later in the summer. There was some confusion about the number of guests and some of the details of the dinner, which seemed to be common, resolvable problems. A key issue to remember, however, is that Jacob likes calm. His preference is to avoid conflict. Before we knew it, they announced that they had gone to the Justice of the Peace with her father and her aunt as witnesses. My husband and I were flabbergasted! Jacob's father was as well.

Jacob and Rachel seemed to be very happy and excited about their decision. I must admit that I was disappointed that they didn't have a bigger wedding, but it was hard not to be happy for them. The elopement was a way to take personal control of a situation that often has too many outside influencers. They avoided confrontations and it worked for them.

The best part of his marriage to Rachel was the increased self-confidence and contentment that she seemed to inspire in him. He was definitely happier and more relaxed having a partner and a loving relationship. They really enjoyed being with each other. Over the years they have developed a healthy dependency on one another and they have maintained a respect for each other's strengths.

Even though Rachel knew that Jacob had schizophrenia, she may not have realized at the time that their marriage would be so complicated by his illness. Early in the relationship, they experienced problems with communication and understanding that went beyond typical newlywed adjustments. As his dependency on her grew, he became fearful that she would leave him.

It was hard for him to go somewhere without her and not worry that she would still be there for him when he returned. For instance, if he stopped by our house without her, he would be constantly texting her. Trying to have an ordinary conversation with him was maddening, as his face was always in his phone. He had trouble concentrating on anything else whenever he was not with her. I would imagine work was a struggle for him as well. Somehow, they plowed through these overwhelming trust issues. Eventually she was able to reassure him of her commitment and he was able to accept with more certainty that the relationship was solid for both of them.

From a psychological perspective, there were probably many contributing factors. His previous relationship with Sally had left him vulnerable. His desire for closeness and his fear of abandonment due to family divorce may have been a factor. His need for excessive reassurance may also be related to the psychological theory that consistency and permanence or security is especially important to individuals with schizophrenia. As mentioned earlier, schizophrenia can create internal chaos. Finding external structure provides a sense of stability and comfort. Whatever the issue, his fantasies scared him. Rachel was not planning to leave him. Even though it is hard to know what was inside his head, constant checking on his wife's whereabouts characterized their early marriage.

The good news is that over time they developed trust and experienced the personal growth that comes from having a partner. They have created realistic goals and expectations for themselves. Rachel has become a helpful, consistent figure in his recovery. She provides emotional support and daily structure for him and, in general, is very nurturing. The relationship benefits are also balanced. He finds meaning that reaches beyond himself by committing himself to the role of caretaker for her and for her disabled brother, Terry. He has moved much of his dependency needs from my husband and me to his wife, which is an appropriate milestone development. In addition, he has become more independent, in general, in the process of caring for Rachel and Terry. They have created a healthy interdependence within their new family system.

At this point my role began to change. Until he and Rachel got married, I had always met his psychologist or his psychiatrist. That didn't mean that I participated in every appointment, but I did have a chance to meet his doctors and share my perspective when needed or asked. My initial research emphasized that involvement of family members in the treatment process was beneficial (Smerud & Rosenfarb, 2011). In generations past, when families were considered the source of schizophrenia, psychotherapists wanted them out of the picture. It may be true also that in the past relatives dropped off their loved ones with serious mental illness at asylums and may never have returned for them. During much of the 20th century, few mental health treatment interventions were effective. Patients may have been abandoned because families had no idea what to do and felt hopeless, while being left behind may have heightened the anger and symptoms of patients who needed care and consistency. The history of mental health treatment is filled with many horror stories. Both physicians and families felt that people with schizophrenia were doomed and for many years they really were. I certainly did not want to send a message of abandonment or doom. In order to facilitate his progress in whatever way I could, I remained involved for many years.

Fortunately, by the time Jacob was diagnosed, parents and family members were encouraged to be part of the treatment team. Newer research found that the more relatives learned about the illness and its treatment, and the longer they remained involved in the recovery process, the more the patient benefitted and their prognosis improved. Family involvement means symptom improvement, fewer relapses and a stronger connection (Smerud & Rosenfarb, 2011). This certainly had been one of our goals. We found it helpful for all of us to learn as much as we could about Jacob's illness. We also tried to find ways to be emotionally supportive. It was important for him to have advocates who could seek out community resources to help with the process of independence. We also wanted to make sure that Jacob took his medications consistently and got to his appointments. We became aware of relapse warning signs and developed a plan if and when a setback occurred. Hopefully, our involvement helped Jacob in the way that research suggested.

Once Jacob got married, though, it seemed appropriate for me to step back. He really didn't need me to micromanage his appointments; even before he got married, he kept his own schedule without difficulty. What I really didn't need to do anymore was tag along each time he met a new psychiatrist or psychotherapist. His wife became a good helpmate, and I had already created a timeline for him to share with his treatment team. Now, Rachel inherited the job, adding to the timeline as doctors or treatment needs changed.

Keeping a history of his treatment was really useful for psychiatrists and therapists. The timeline was a simple sequence of events, on which I noted when Jacob was first diagnosed, what medications he had taken, and what psychological interventions had been tried. The timeline also indicated what results or side effects occurred when he was taking a medication. Jacob's timeline can follow him and aid his memory as he engages new psychiatrists or treatments. Because his symptoms might not end, his treatment might need to be lifelong as well. His doctors and therapists sometimes move or retire or change insurance plans. Also, his symptoms may not be so debilitating at times and so regularly scheduled psychiatric appointments may not be as frequent, and psychotherapy may not be as necessary. When he experiences excessive stress, the importance of professional treatment intensifies. Keeping track of his treatment can be helpful when making transitions. I passed this baton to Rachel.

In fact, changes to most of his treatment team began soon after he got married, as he no longer qualified for my husband's insurance plan. At first, he transferred to his employer's plan. When he changed jobs to use his computer skills, he often worked as a contract employee. These jobs were time-limited without benefits. Thankfully, Ohio was one of the states that added Medicaid expansion. He was able to have good insurance even though his employment was not consistent. He was also able to get good psychiatric and psychological help through the county mental health programs, and his medications were free.

So now, with these major steps forward, could we sit back and relax? No, at least not yet. A blip – not a full-blown relapse – occurred in 2016. Because he had developed arm tremors, his psychiatrist decided to switch medications. He had been on Abilify for at least six years or more and tremors were a possible side effect for some users. As soon as he stopped Abilify and began taking a different medication his tremors subsided. Even better, this new medication seemed to be miraculous. His voices, which had always lurked in the remote recesses of his mind, completely disappeared. With other medications, the voices were only subdued. Jacob was elated. He enjoyed more energy and seemed to be able to work well.

In addition, he was happily employed. He really liked where he was consulting and hoped that this work assignment as a technology consultant would become permanent. He derived a lot of pleasure from his work challenges and his associates. He took the risk of sharing his diagnosis with his supervisors so that he could request accommodations. The company had been willing to adapt office protocol to fit his special needs, such as allowing him to move around or pace when he was on the phone. He was also able to use earbuds for music to improve his focus. Prior to the new medication, the music helped to block out voices that would become louder when stressed. Most of his technical contract employers allowed these helpful adjustments. The American with Disabilities Act of 1990 prohibits discrimination in the workplace and requires employment accommodations just as it did in his academic settings.

Unfortunately, what seemed like a long-awaited breakthrough turned into a downslide. One of the side effects that he experienced with the new medication was increased agitation. His once mild-mannered demeanor changed to increasing irritation and temper outbursts at home. Rachel described him as more argumentative and defensive. Most likely this agitation contributed to hi job loss. During that time, he posted a news article on the company's group chat about a mass murder in a nearby area of Ohio. He said that he wanted to warn co-workers who may have lived in that area. Evidently, he was not supposed to use that venue for non-work-related posts. In addition, a few co-workers who did not know Jacob very well were concerned because they viewed his post as a threat rather than a concern. His supervisor dismissed him on the spot for violating company rules. Jacob felt misunderstood and became unusually upset and angry. At that point he had to pack up his desk and leave. His psychiatrist was willing to write a letter in his defense, but the situation appeared to be unchangeable. His doctor immediately changed his prescription to Rexulti, a form of Abilify, which worked much better than either of the other two medications and definitely did not agitate him.

Eventually life began to look better again. Not long after, he actually found a direct hire technology job that was permanent and had benefits. It was also located only ten minutes from his home. He enjoys his role, his colleagues and his schedule. He often socializes with friends at work. At present he and his wife are now finding ways to make ends meet and budget their money. They have debt from past learning experiences but a plan to get themselves on the path to better credit. I can observe a sense of calmness and happiness growing within him. Two more goals are now within reach: financial independence and career contentment.

One more big game-changer has occurred recently: financing a home! With some help for a down payment, Jacob and Rachel found a condo that was perfect for them. The main living areas are on the first floor, which makes it possible for Terry to get around easier. The lower level gives them a private family room, storage and laundry. The front has a nice deck next to a well-manicured, shared green space. To put it mildly, they seem overjoyed with this move. The extra square footage allows them to comfortably entertain their friends and family more too. An added bonus is that it is even closer to Jacob's present job. Overall, it was a considerable step forward. What a relief to me, as well, to see them more settled and also to have all of their boxes out of our basement!

The question is, of course, "What will the future bring and how will he manage his illness?" If the past is any predictor of the future, he will continue to move toward his goals. He may have more blips, but they will most likely be surmountable. What both he and I have had to realize is that his illness has set him back with regard to expectations or developmental milestones compared to his peers. It is true that many of his high school and college contemporaries are working career jobs and have started families. Many may be in better circumstances financially. Yet most individuals with a serious illness, whether mental or physical, usually have to find their own pace, and that is what he is doing. It is important to remember that the same persistence and stubbornness that he most likely inherited from his mother will continue to propel him forward. And even without a serious illness, many people jump off the beaten path and find their own way.

CHAPTER 8

COPING WITH

SCHIZOPHRENIC "LEFTOVERS"

After 20 years, does Jacob still have any leftover symptoms of schizophrenia? Yes. Schizophrenia has never completely disappeared for him, and does not for many people. Learning to cope with symptoms at various stages of treatment has been important, and such strategies can be a focus of client–therapist counseling. Learning what works and what doesn't is sometimes trial and error, especially since symptoms and their leftovers vary from one person to another and from one phase of the illness to the next. As a parent I have found it helpful to just ask Jacob directly what he is experiencing and what, if anything, he needs at the moment.

Jacob, like most individuals with schizophrenia, has never exhibited all of the symptoms listed in the *Diagnostic and Statistical Manual V*. He has never had visual hallucinations, but he did have and still can hear voices, otherwise known as auditory hallucinations. Overall, he is not paranoid or distrustful of others, except when he was first married. In fact, sometimes he may be too trustful. The disorganized thinking and behaviors as reflected in his academic writing have disappeared. His speech is fine and his communication skills are very good. Occasionally, his feelings can be flat or hard to detect, either due to his medication or because he's tired. He often exhibits little or no energy, especially in comparison to his hyperactive childhood, though his prescriptions could also be contributing to this as well.

Fortunately, he does not suffer from tremors or tardive dyskinesia (TD), which can happen as a result of using some antipsychotics for long periods of time. TD can cause repetitive, involuntary body movements, facial grimacing and tongue thrusting. Usually, when these side effects begin, they are lifelong. Once or twice in the past Jacob began to develop a tic or tremor, but his psychiatrist quickly switched him to a different medication. New pharmaceuticals are marketed regularly and are often improvements of earlier antipsychotics. Whenever he needs to switch medications for any reason, the change is most often a positive one.

Basically, Jacob has learned many useful coping skills and his medication can control many of the symptoms that are leftover problems. For example, with regard to auditory hallucinations, his newer prescription seems to be much better at keeping the voices at bay, which can still hurl their ugly taunts, especially when he is stressed. The voices can be highly irritating distractions that surface when he experiences excessive pressure from work, relationships or finances, but listening to music has been a useful coping strategy. In the past when he visited us, he used to walk into the house and go directly to the room where we kept the stereo. He would always tune it to a classical music station for soothing music. This music reduces his discomfort and blocks out inner noises. While he was in college, a very good friend of mine gave him an iPod to help him while he was on campus. Now, with newer technology, he relies on his phone or his Bluetooth headphones. I hardly ever see him without something connected to his ear. As noted earlier, his employers permit special accommodations at work for music as well.

Another negative symptom that hangs around is withdrawal. If the situation becomes too tense or he expects extraordinary pressure at the outset, he finds comfortable exit strategies or avoids certain settings in the first place. In the recent past, Jacob has been uncomfortable with some of our large family gatherings. If he is in a good place, he may show up, but if not, he will stay home. Just a few months ago he did attend a welcome home party for one of his nephews in the Navy, which included a large gathering of extended relatives and friends. This is the first time in several years that many of these family members have seen Jacob, and he appeared to feel quite welcomed as he engaged in conversations with them. I took that as a barometer of his present state.

Adaptations and accommodations appear to be situation-dependent. Jacob has consciously or unconsciously learned what settings are manageable for him. His wife reports that even though he wants to go to the family gatherings at his father's house, her aunt's and even mine, he often gets overwhelmed. This usually results in escape-sleeping on a couch or chair until it is time to go home. What is particularly interesting is that even though his eyes are closed and he appears to be zoned out, he usually hears everything we say. When we start to talk about him, a big smile will grow across his face and he will sometimes open his eyes.

Recently, we invited Jacob and Rachel for lunch to show them our pictures from a trip to Costa Rica. This was only a gathering for the four of us. While most acquaintances would politely tolerate our photos, he slipped into a semi-coma on the couch after the second or third picture. He insisted that he was listening to everything we said. Actually, when we quizzed him, he was right. He was paying attention, but his eyes were closed. Was it overwhelming for him to think about our trip? Was it really that dull and he wasn't assertive enough to tell us? I could believe that he was bored, but he denied that was the case. Was it his medication? My guess is that it is his way of escaping, but there is no way to really know the reason for his need to get away. He just does. Rachel says that she is always apologizing for his "comas".

Remember my earlier stories about his hyperactivity? Well, I actually long for some of that now. Jacob often is plagued by inertia or low motivation, additional negative symptoms associated with schizophrenia, and he has been experimenting with various strategies to overcome this sluggishness. One of his present goals is to complete a computer certification to boost his career. Preparing for the test requires much reading and memorizing, and that takes a lot of focus and drive on his part. He identified the best time period for him to read was late at night. He gets home from work after 9pm, eats, spends time with his wife, plays video games, or has wind-down time of some kind. After that he planned to read his certification study manual until 2am or so. The time is quiet with few distractions. His plan looked reasonable. He based it on his schedule of staying up late and waking up late, since he doesn't start work until noon. In truth, it is similar to a pattern that I used in graduate school to find a quiet, distraction-free time to study. The experiment was worth trying, but it only lasted a few weeks. He either got too tired or he lost interest in pursuing that certification – or both.

Jacob may have schizophrenia, but he is definitely tenacious! Based on what he learned from Plan A, he has now created Plan B. First, he researched certifications and decided that he wanted to pursue a different one that had more potential for him. Now his new plan is to still study after a late dinner and when the house is quiet. He also discovered that he reads books electronically easier than printed books. The new certification manual that he is studying is electronic.

Routine and consistency are helpful for him. Working, sleeping and getting up at approximately the same time every day provides a sense of security and comfort. This goes back to the psychological dynamic that psychotic experiences are frightening and lead to feeling out of control. Generating structure can pull those fears back into line. When he gets off-track, his wife is a good coordinator for him. Most of the time she is able to encourage him to maintain his routine. Early in their relationship, when Jacob would struggle more with lethargic symptoms, she would frantically call me asking, "Help me get Jacob out of bed. He is going to be late for work." We would then brainstorm together to come up with a plan. Oftentimes it meant making an appointment with his psychiatrist or increasing the frequency of his psychotherapy. Those were frustrating times for her and for me, but, fortunately, we haven't had to deal with this type of issue for a number of years.

Self-care has been another stumbling block at times. One of the negative symptoms, inertia or low energy, can stand in the way of good grooming and hygiene. There may still be times when he sleeps too late to get a shower before work. Sometimes he doesn't brush his teeth for a long period of time. Other times his hair is unkempt. Even though the stubble look is fashionable, Jacob may take it too far. The good news is that this is not 100 percent of the time. When it does occur, though, I suspect that it can get in the way socially and professionally. He has said that he addresses these behaviors sometimes when he is in therapy. His wife does her best to nag him when she needs to help him get back to a more wholesome image, and this strategy must work for them. My impression is that Jacob actually appreciates her nagging and labels it as her love and concern. He does his best to cooperate. During his visits in the past, I would occasionally drive him to a nearby hair salon. He always seemed to welcome the haircut, so I wasn't making him do something that he opposed doing. Recently he has been more likely to do this for himself.

Has my parenting style changed over the years? Hopefully, it has. I often thought of writing a book on how to parent adult children! In our situation, tact, diplomacy, directness and flexibility have become essential parts of my repertoire. Adaptability – picking and choosing priorities – is something all parents need whether they have a disabled child or not. Weighing choices is important. For instance, is it more critical for him to shave his stubble or enjoy a relaxed meal with my husband and me? Facial hair can be trendy, right? Having a positive relationship usually wins.

Additionally, acceptance and love are paramount keys to parenting. I can't make Jacob perfect and he can't make me perfect. I love him for who he is and because he is my son. He is a human manifestation on this planet who does his best and his best can be amazing. I love him with and without his schizophrenic symptoms. I love his sameness and I love his uniqueness. Jacob is who he is.

That being said, I often wish that Jacob could be more confident and assertive. Over the years he has been fairly self-assured but just not consistently. When he goes through bad times or is overwhelmed by his symptoms, his lack of confidence may be more related to sadness or depression. It must be hard to feel you are doing your best or that life is going well when voices in your head tell you otherwise. His self-esteem may also falter at times when comparing himself to peers who may be further along in careers or "adulting". Those are the times that I wish I could be a voice in his head saying, "But, Jacob, you are doing well. Look at all you have accomplished and how far you have come. Look at who you are as a person. You are very smart; you are very sensitive and caring; your values and your character are admirable. Your spirit of kindness inspires all of us. What more do you need?" That's the voice I would like him to develop!

His assertiveness is growing but his passivity still takes over sometimes. Being honest and forthright is something that he struggled with as early as third grade when his father and I divorced. It was easier then to act out in anger than be direct. He has certainly outgrown the misbehaving part, but he still has a hard time stating what he wants. Because he is sensitive, he may worry about hurting feelings. I also think he is afraid of others' reactions, i.e., will they say no? Will they get mad? Will they worry about him? No matter how much we may discuss this issue in our relationship, he is still an expert at avoiding direct confrontations. Over the years I have tried my best to learn to react less impulsively and to be more accepting, but I am not the only one with whom he covers up or has trouble talking to honestly.

Thank goodness for texting. It has provided an avenue for him to say what he feels or to tell me what he really wants. Many times, we can have what appear to be good conversations either on the phone or in person. For example, we could be chatting and he tells me, "Everything is great. Nothing new has happened. Work is fine." After we hang up, within ten minutes, he will text saying, "By the way, we just got another dog," or "My car is making strange noises." Texting also helps me filter my frustrations and allows me to respond appropriately. I almost always dread texts that I receive right after we hang up, as they usually reveal the real reason that he called or wanted to talk.

Maybe he needs another positive inner voice that says, "Jacob, you are an adult. You can get another dog if you want. Also, it is okay to ask for help. You may not get exactly what you want to hear all the time, but you can handle it." Right after helping him move into his new condo, he did give me a welcome surprise. He texted me on the way home, and my first thought was, *Oh no, what could be wrong?* When I got the courage to look at my phone, he had typed, "Thank you so much." I smile every time I think about that.

Most likely, Jacob needs much encouragement in the form of verbal and emotional support. Even though he claims that his most negative voices have taken a back seat, he still holds back or doesn't trust himself. One day, while driving home from work, I was listening to an interview on NPR on "Here and Now". Someone from the American Disabilities Association explained that many people who have a mental illness disability lack confidence in the workplace. The most important part of her message related to stress and symptom management. She said that many individuals with mental illness refrain from advancing their careers and settle for lower-level jobs for fear that pressure from more advanced positions will make their symptoms worse. She pointed out that while stress can increase symptoms, it can occur with most jobs regardless of level. The key is learning stress management techniques rather than trying to find the elusive job with no stress. Most likely the experience of being underemployed compounds the fear that you can't move up since the stress even at this level does not seem manageable. Good psychotherapy could be an important ingredient to career confidence and satisfaction for Jacob and for many in his situation.

During this past year Jacob was feeling bad because he had again fallen behind with his work-related deadlines. Even when he would catch up for a period of time, he would always lose ground again. His supervisors worked with him to develop a plan to get up to speed and, importantly, to remain there. My husband, who spent the latter part of his career in the computer software field, explained to him that was a fairly normal pattern, to have a lull followed by high demand times. He didn't think that Jacob should be so hard on himself. Normalizing work experiences and stresses may be a helpful stress-management approach. Knowing that happens with many people in the field makes it easier for him to continue to search for solutions rather than feeling discouraged and giving up. Research suggests that individuals with schizophrenia can stigmatize themselves, thus negatively impacting their self-esteem and self-trust (Brohan et al., 2009 & Horsselenburg et al., 2016). In this situation, lacking self-trust means that he inaccurately assumes his excessive accumulation of open tickets or some other work-related problem is related to schizophrenia and that there is nothing that he can do in order to change or impact the outcome. The NPR interview was actually referring to this kind of self-stigma which negatively influences job performance. Jacob often consciously or unconsciously experiences self-stigma and holds himself back by underestimating what he is able to do.

Is there a simple, magic answer? The treatment and recovery process would be so much easier if there was. Reading, sharing with others and trying new interventions in order to determine what helps has been part of the healing process. Even after a plateau has been reached, upheavals can occur and new interventions may be necessary. My son has had only one major relapse, but he has had many less intense setbacks. Setbacks are not uncommon and planning for them can be helpful. Some may be short-lived and require only a minimal amount of time to recover, while others take longer.

Do I worry about what will happen to Jacob after we die? That is a common fear for most parents with sons or daughters with disabilities. Jacob is lucky to have a caring wife and a sister who will always be there for him. We also have a solid extended family that includes stepsiblings. Emotionally, the bases are covered. I worry most about his finances. What if he has a setback to his regular income and no one is able to help him?

Some parents are able to set up trust funds and perhaps Health Savings Accounts, but those options may not be financially possible for everyone. Recently, the state of Ohio adopted a financial planning resource for families with children who have disabilities. In 2016 I received a letter from my state representative describing a bill that she co-sponsored and was proud to say was signed into law. This law was designed to help Ohioans with special needs establish a 529A or

State Achieving a Better Life Experience (STABLE) account, similar to the 529 college account. It is a federally tax-advantaged savings account for individuals with disabilities or for their loved ones to save money for them without them losing their government disability benefits. You can open an account with as little as $50.00 and can put in as much as $14,000 annually. The funds can be directed to mutual funds available to the account or to an FDIC-insured savings account. The funds can be used for a variety of expenses that improve the quality of Jacob's life including living expenses, housing, education and training, transportation, health, legal fees and financial management. Thanks to STABLE, I was able to save enough while I was working to help him with a down payment for the purchase of a condo. Hopefully I will to be able to continue to contribute now that I am retired even though my deposits will be smaller. Even though my savings do not amount to enough to create a trust fund for future needs, this STABLE account will provide for some of his unforeseen living expenses.

Finding solutions to schizophrenia symptoms or problems related to the condition is a lifelong process. As with any journey, the beginning is usually the most stressful part. It's a time for preparing, trying to anticipate what to expect, organizing and planning for the events on the itinerary, and getting to the destination. Once you arrive or start the trip, much of the hard part is over. With schizophrenia, it took months and years for Jacob to arrive at a place that seemed stable. Then, of course, as in most trips, unexpected challenges occurred, but we figured them out. Most journeys, however, bring you home again, back to the beginning, where everything is the same as when you started. This is where the metaphor breaks down. In the case of schizophrenia, the journey does not usually take you back to how things used to be. Arriving home may be a relief, but it may not look the same.

In an editorial in *The New York Times*, David Brooks addressed the idea of change and used an image that is appropriate for describing the beauty that can be found in it. His friend and artist Makoto Fujimura introduced him to Kintsugi bowls made of ceramic that were approximately 3,000–4,000 years old. What seemed to make them so beautiful was the manner in which they were restored. Some time ago they had been broken into shards. During the 15th century, a Japanese artist glued them back together using lacquer and gold. Their glimmering veins made them even more valuable and stunning. That is not to say that Jacob was not a beautiful young man before his journey with schizophrenia, but his experiences and his growth have added depth to his beauty. I am ever so grateful that he is my son.

CHAPTER 9

RECOVERY

Will Jacob ever recover? The answer is yes, though my answer to that question has evolved over time. Initially, successful recovery to me meant that in a very short period of time after starting his medication, Jacob would have no symptoms. He would soon be back to normal and do everything that everyone else his age was doing. As mentioned earlier, my first reaction to Jacob's diagnosis was to continue as usual. I thought, *He just needs to keep going without any interruptions in his development, in his schooling, in his personal growth. Perhaps all this is just a passing illness and he will be fine soon.* At that time, I was hoping that we would find the magic medication that would take away all his symptoms. Part of that was a denial: surely it was just a bad dream? Part of it was simply confusion. At the beginning of our journey, I knew very few people with schizophrenia.

During the early part of my career, few individuals diagnosed with schizophrenia sought psychotherapy with psychologists in private practice, nor did their parents. I had one client, a young man, who became symptomatic in high school. He spent a short time at a children's hospital for evaluation and medical intervention. He lived with his grandparents. His grandmother was appropriately involved in his treatment and appeared to be realistic about what he could accomplish until the medication regimen was established. She helped him get academic help outside of the traditional school setting and moved with him to a different city, at which point we lost touch.

She appeared to be making healthy decisions for her grandson and he seemed to benefit from her active involvement.

The only other experience with schizophrenia that I can recall prior to Jacob's diagnosis was an academic rotation in a state hospital in Missouri in 1971. The patient, diagnosed with catatonic symptoms of schizophrenia, was bedridden. She was immobile and posed in a very uncomfortable position. As she laid in bed, her right leg was lifted and bent, and both arms were held out in a distorted fashion. The staff provided slings for her limbs to rest, although her muscles appeared to be rigid. She was the "challenge" of the hospital. This was, of course, long before any really good medications were available. No one, including myself, a very green master's student at the time, could rouse her. I often think how sad her life was and how wasted her time was, posed so woodenly in that position. Who knows, but perhaps if she had been born 20 years later, she might have been more functional?

Certainly, my graduate school training in the 70s did not paint an encouraging picture. Most available treatments had many side effects that were just about as bad as schizophrenia. Separation from "schizophrenogenic families" was encouraged. Medications were advancing but not yet as effective as present formulations. Patients were heavily sedated, which decreased their motivation even more, and thought processing was diminished. This was considered a step forward from pre-medication days, however, when nothing really seemed to help active hallucinations and disorganized thoughts. No wonder so many people feared not just the diagnosis, but the treatment as well.

In my spare time I enjoy reading about English history. In the 15th century, King Henry VI most likely suffered from schizophrenia (Bark, 2002). In his early years he was an active and ambitious king. During his late 20s and early 30s, however, he became more paranoid and began to fall into long periods of catatonia. After months of "sleeping", he would awaken for periods of time. Once he was alert, his behavior was more passive and he displayed little interest in his royal responsibilities. He appeared to have lost touch with reality and seemed to experience auditory hallucinations. Like many people with schizophrenia, he became mild-mannered and very vulnerable. The king was easily controlled by his counselors and cousins who wanted his throne. Experts believe that the War of the Roses, or Cousins War, would never have occurred if Henry had not developed schizophrenia. His illness interfered with his ability to defend his throne.

In the search for a recovery model, I found frightening statistics even in the current literature. Not only might Jacob be vulnerable to control or abuse by others, but his chances of dying from suicide are also high. The suicide rate is 8.5 times greater for someone with schizophrenia than in the general population. Between 20 and 50 percent of people with schizophrenia make suicide attempts. Vulnerability is greatest during the initial stages of diagnosis and when depression or substance abuse is associated with symptoms (Kasckow et al., 2011). What I was learning was that recovery from schizophrenia can be considered purely survival. Unfortunately, not everyone makes it.

Hollywood has provided examples of recovery as well by honoring well-known individuals who struggled with schizophrenia, including John Nash and Nathaniel Ayers. The movie *A Beautiful Mind* depicts the former, a brilliant mathematician, as he gradually begins his journey with paranoid schizophrenia. Although he achieves professional recognition with a Nobel Prize for his creative work on game theory, he had difficulty throughout his life with hallucinations. Because he did not like the effects of the early antipsychotic medications, he pushed through his illness often without them. His brilliance and perseverance gave him intermittent years of productivity.

The movie *The Soloist* is a true story as well. Nathaniel Ayers was a child cello prodigy who drops out of Julliard School of Music after two years because of schizophrenia symptoms. His paranoia leads him to homelessness in Los Angeles, where he is discovered by a journalist. He hears and sees Nathaniel on the street beautifully playing a violin with only two strings. The journalist helps him obtain a cello, introduces him to a musician who tries to rehabilitate Nathaniel through music, and also reconnects him with his sister. But Nathaniel does not become a professional cellist as the journalist had hoped. Instead, he joins a street community in Los Angeles called LAMP, which seeks to help people with severe mental illness. At the end of the movie, he is learning to play the guitar, not the cello.

These true stories contributed to my confusion about the definition of recovery. Does it mean being symptom-free or finding a way to make a positive difference in the world as a "good person"? Henry VI, John Nash and Nathaniel Ayers all made contributions that influenced others. Despite Henry VI's confusion and passivity, he founded Eton College, King's College, Cambridge College and All Souls' College, Oxford. John Nash made brilliant contributions to the field of mathematics. In contrast to Henry and John, Nathaniel did not achieve the musical fame that he could have, but he profoundly impacted those who met him. Success does not have to include monumental legacies. Even without schizophrenia, these stories are the exception. It would be great if Jacob could just find his own unique way to make a contribution to the world while coping with his symptoms.

One of the standards that has given me future hope is based on the recovery of Fred Frese, PhD, a psychologist in Ohio who coped with schizophrenia after a diagnosis in his mid-20s. His video presentation (Frese & Frese, 1991) about his journey is inspirational and hopeful. Just knowing that someone with a similar illness was able to overcome the obstacles presented by schizophrenia and, in addition, was able to make such important contributions to the field of serious mental illness has been encouraging. He became a spokesperson and advocate as well as a teacher, clinician and researcher, and I have had the privilege of hearing him present at a statewide workshop. I thought as a mother and a psychologist how grateful I was for his persistence and work. He set a benchmark for what can be achieved despite his challenges. With that in mind, I am not convinced that Jacob had fully unfolded. It felt possible that he would continue to find old abilities returning and new ones still developing that would help him become the person that he wanted to be.

As time went on, we discovered that the recovery process is more complicated and varies from person to person. Figuring out what was going to help Jacob cope with his illness appeared to be more realistic than expecting total remission. One of the keys in my son's improvement was to find the right medication. He tried many formulas initially. His work with his psychiatrist was not a one-stop medical appointment. In fact, it took quite a long time. Even though he still has his medications re-evaluated every few months, changing prescriptions is less common now. He may go for years with a particular regimen. Medication for him continues to be an essential contributor to his improvement.

There are patients and doctors who claim medication is not necessary during the recovery process. One well-known proponent of a more natural treatment, Daniel Fisher, MD, PhD, and his associates developed the National Empowerment Community, treating individuals with serious mental illness, including schizophrenia, without medication. The program is called PACE, Personal Assistance in Community Existence. In the 1990s and early 2000s, they created methods of recovery from schizophrenia based on holistic health and alternative therapies, which were controlled by the patients themselves rather than a clinician. They believe that providing a supportive community and empowering individuals to oversee their recovery needs can in itself be healing. Many of their ideas of empowerment and acceptance have been incorporated into present-day psychotherapy and treatment protocols in most settings. Personally, as a psychologist and a mother, I am more comfortable with an emphasis on strength- building rather illness-reinforcing. I have been, however, reluctant for Jacob to take the chance of seeking recovery without medication. Some people may want to explore this option, but for me, it was too painful to risk seeing my son possibly tortured by his auditory hallucinations again. While there may be some conflicting research about medication, in Jacob's case the benefits outweigh the risks. For his part, Jacob has been committed to taking his medication regularly. The choice has been his to make.

The other good news is that recently emerging research and treatment practices may help him manage his symptoms even better.

While he has found the medication that works best for him now, newer pharmaceuticals are on the horizon. While most present options can reduce hallucinations and thought disorders, they have limited impact on emotional expression, social interest and attention difficulties – these leftover symptoms that can still plague some individuals with schizophrenia. Jacob continues to struggle with attention problems. In addition, even the newer generation of medications have side effects, especially after lengthy use, which is why Jacob changes medications from time to time. Research in the areas of the neural dynamics and schizophrenia are producing new insights and pathways for targeting most of the symptoms, the active and the passive, with fewer side effects (Stepnicki et al., 2018). It is comforting to remember that he and others with a diagnosis of schizophrenia have science on their side.

The truth is that not only can schizophrenic symptoms vary from one person to another, but the disease itself can evolve and remit in varied ways. While there really is no cure at this point for schizophrenia, symptoms can dissipate for many. Jacob's can disappear from his daily experience and remain in remission until he encounters an excessively stressful event. Studies done before the advent of antipsychotic medications indicate that 20 percent of patients recovered independently while 80 percent did not. More recent research has found that 60 percent of individuals diagnosed with schizophrenia achieve remission, which means having no or few symptoms for a period of six months. The mathematician John Nash claimed his condition began to improve about 20 years after onset and 30 years later believed he was free of symptoms or irrational thinking without medication (Rettner, 2015).

In 2009, Dr Rashmi Nemadi and Dr Mark Dombeck published an article on recovery timelines. They found that ten years after discovery and treatment, 50 percent of people diagnosed with schizophrenia are recovered enough to live independently; 25 percent are improved but need a strong social support network; and 15 percent remain unimproved. Unfortunately, the other 10 percent eventually succumb to suicide. Studies also show that 30 years on from diagnosis, the situation is similar, except that more people become independent and 5 percent more commit suicide. For parents or caregivers who are feeling discouraged, seeing a strong statistical trend favoring independence is hopeful. My husband and I have been encouraged by Jacob's growing independence. Years ago, Glen was psychologically preparing for Jacob to be with us for the rest of our lives. While that still can be what some families experience, the majority of individuals with schizophrenia can manage their own affairs.

Even more exciting is the American Psychological Association initiative, Recovery to Practice, which provides resources and training for professionals working with individuals who have serious mental illness including schizophrenia. Rather than focusing on the pathology of schizophrenia, psychologists now have an opportunity to learn how to help clients recover or develop skills once the acute symptoms have been treated. A 15-module training program has been developed to teach psychology students how to understand and facilitate the recovery process. The field of psychology has grown enormously since I was in graduate school and continues to offer hope for Jacob's ability to become the person he wants to be (Clay, 2014).

Factors that helped in Jacob's recovery process included early identification and treatment, good family and social support, and avoidance of street medications and alcohol. These are factors that can be controlled to a certain extent. Shortly after Jacob diagnosed himself and his flagrant symptoms were apparent to us, he saw a psychiatrist for an evaluation. A thorough medical examination is important too in order to rule out other possible problems that sometimes look like schizophrenia, such as a thyroid disorder, acute porphyria and autoimmune deficiencies, to name a few possibilities (Freudenreich, 2012). The immediacy of medical attention contributed to his progress. The shorter the period of time between intense symptom manifestation and antipsychotic medication, the greater the odds of remission. His initial treatment reduced severe symptoms of auditory hallucinations and confused thinking.

Continued psychological counseling helped him develop coping strategies. Recent research (Mucci et al., 2021) found that improving cognitive training and psychosocial interventions and linking them to real-life functioning improved recovery. Therapy during these early months helped Jacob identify ways to understand and counteract messages from his voices. His psychologist kept a watch on his suicidal thoughts and helped him monitor his emotional reactions. He learned about his illness and the impact it was having on his present functioning. With her help, he was able to work, attend college, and develop supportive friendships.

While we were not perfect, we did our best to provide family support, another factor that positively improves schizophrenic symptoms. We made sure that he had the resources that he needed for recovery such as medication, psychological counseling, a place to live, food to eat and an accepting atmosphere. It was scary for him as his world began to fall apart and he wasn't sure what to do about it. Giving him consistent family presence and involvement was something effective that we could do. In addition, being his advocate and helping him navigate the treatment world was an important family role. His confusion and distortions made finding the help he needed on his own very challenging. Research supports what we learned from experience: families and caregivers can be a cornerstone of the recovery process (Smerud & Rosenfarb, 2011).

Today many individuals diagnosed with schizophrenia get the care that they need thanks to family support and involvement. Others find assistance in hospitals, nursing homes and group homes. About 6 percent end up in the legal system and may receive treatment that way. Another 6 percent live on the streets or in homeless shelters (Torrey, 2019). Paranoia that accompanies some schizophrenia can make it hard for family and mental health professionals to intervene. Also, some individuals are not aware that they are exhibiting symptoms and may be resistant to treatment. Legally, no one can be forced into it unless they are at risk of harming themselves or others. We were grateful that Jacob wanted help. We did not find it necessary to seek professional consultation or develop strategies to encourage him to get him into treatment. He strongly desired interventions.

I am also grateful that Jacob has never, to my knowledge, used alcohol or street drugs. He didn't make those choices in high school or college and seemed to socialize with friends who made similar decisions. Because individuals who develop schizophrenia are more likely to suffer from substance abuse, the chances that he would use were higher than the general population. If he had, his treatment would have been compromised. Marijuana, other street drugs and alcohol can increase schizophrenic symptoms such as hallucinatory experiences and can decrease the effectiveness of medications (Winklbaur et al., 2006). There are treatment programs for dual diagnosis, but Jacob did not have to use them.

Were there other factors that contributed to his present level of progress? Yes, but many of them are not within an individual's control. One example is genetic transmission. If either his father or I had a diagnosis of schizophrenia, his chances of symptom remission would be more difficult. Namade and Dombeck (2009) report that the recovery process for someone with schizophrenia is easier if they do not have a parent or a sibling with the condition. Because of the increased risk for fathers or mothers with schizophrenia to have children who develop it, too, my son and his wife have made the decision not to have children. This was one way that they could take control of the genetic side of his illness.

Not having children of their own was certainly a difficult choice for them, but they thoroughly considered the risk. Once they decided, they were unsure how to tell me. Because they know how much I love being a grandmother, they expected me to be very upset and try to talk them out of it. Truthfully, I believe they made a wise choice. Raising children can be stressful and expensive even without the complication of one parent having schizophrenia. Instead, they are nurturing pet-owners. They take good care of my grand-dog, three grand-cats, two grand-hamsters and one grand-cockatiel. They love their grand-zoo and so do I!

Although Jacob and Rachel have ruled out having biological children, they see adoption and foster care as a possible direction, as they do love to be with children. They enjoy time with their nieces and nephews, and Rachel helps a friend who is a single parent by taking care of her little girl who is about six years old. She frequently spends the night with them and they enjoy taking her to nearby parks or special entertainment venues. This is a less stressful way to enjoy parenting and works well for them now.

In addition, Jacob's functioning prior to the onset of schizophrenia had an impact on his symptom improvement. He had already developed good social skills before displaying signs of his illness, which made recovery easier, as he only had to recover skill sets, rather than having to learn them from the beginning. Some people like Jacob who develop the condition were outgoing when they were younger and already had the ability to read social cues and interact with peers in appropriate ways. Because he once had these skills, early warning signs of schizophrenia were also more noticeable. When he began to withdraw, his family and friends questioned the new behavior. In addition, his social abilities enabled him to be open to seeking help and talking to others about his mental health needs.

Jacob's awareness that his thoughts and behavior were unusual also helped propel him to seek help sooner. Maybe he would have even done this on his own. He was most certainly aware of his auditory hallucinations and knew that his thinking was not as it used to be. The way in which this changed his social communication was frightening and confusing to him. He wanted relief from these symptoms and has, since the beginning, faithfully taken medication to avoid relapses. Knowing that medication helped him was another important insight. He has been very reluctant to risk a setback by not taking his medications. Even though many individuals with schizophrenia are not compliant with medications (Torrey, 2019), the outpatient clients that I later saw in my practice felt the same way as Jacob – "I want the medication that will protect me from that confusion and from those voices!"

Research has revealed other factors that can positively influence recovery. For whatever reason, rapid onset of initial symptoms rather than a more gradual change usually means a faster comeback. The same goes for later age of onset instead of teenage onset, being female, and prior normal brain structure and function. Again, these are statistics that predict a pattern for most individuals, but variations occur. It is always important to remember that while these trends may be apparent today, future discoveries may change the entire picture of recovery. Just in the relatively short time since my own graduate school training, the knowledge base about schizophrenia has grown by leaps and bounds.

Do character or personality traits aid or detract from the recovery process? Although there have been no studies on this area of research, my belief is that Jacob's perseverance has been essential to his recovery. His desire to fight his illness has pushed him to positively cope throughout the past 20 years. For example, that first summer when he worked for a local amusement park while coping with the drowsiness from his medication had to have taken much effort. He did his best to try to make it work, and he also pursued several different employment opportunities. At all times, he initiated the interviews and the job changes, and he also drove himself to work, literally and figuratively. During this process he began to learn about how stress affected his symptoms and how to cope with medication's sedating side effects. Even now, he continues to learn what types of technical roles work best for him and what level of stress he can handle. With each new position, he has learned more and more about how to cope and how to work to the best of his ability.

Another important personal strength that may have helped Jacob is his underlying intelligence and ability to discern what's best for him. Although schizophrenia is a thought disorder that oftentimes clouds good reasoning and decision-making, Jacob seemed to retain his ability to see the big picture and figure out what was and wasn't healthy for him. He was able to interact with his case managers at the Bureau of Rehabilitation in order to decide on an academic direction in college. Although he was not sure about future jobs at the time, he knew that he had a love of history. He made positive connections with new friends in the dorm and especially through the Student Disability office. The Student Disability group on campus gave him opportunities to develop leadership skills. He also learned to maneuver city bus schedules so that he could meet regularly with his psychiatrist. He learned how much information to share about his disability with others and navigate relationships with people who may not understand his illness. He figured out the process of graduating from college, being in a committed marriage, and maintaining consistent employment – no small feats for someone struggling with schizophrenia.

Has he achieved all that it is possible for him to achieve? Has he reached his full potential? Maybe. Would he prefer to find career employment that pays more? Would he like to buy a new car or have extra money for leisure activities and a vacation? Are these realistic goals that he can expect to achieve? I have little doubt that he can get to this level of functioning, albeit at his own pace. He works on these goals as I write.

At this point, does my definition of recovery mean that he will be completely symptom-free? I think it is a real possibility, especially if he continues with his medications. He recently told me that he has experienced a remarkable improvement in his symptoms in the past two to three years. Although his voices return when he becomes very anxious, this only occurs a few times a year, and these experiences are short-lived. He has learned how to cope with them and how to use them as red flags to reassess his stress level. When a flare-up occurs, he uses the experience as a guide to understand the source of his discomfort.

He also reports that he feels much more engaged with the world compared to how he felt in college, and even compared to seven or eight years ago. For many years he felt aloof or disconnected, as if he didn't really fit socially or belong to the world. Now he feels much more connected. He still remains in touch with friends from college or past jobs and has made new friends where he works now. Thanks to social media and video games, he interacts with many people, even during the COVID-19 pandemic. He is happy with his present functioning and his engagement with life.

He describes having had an epiphany two to three years ago when he suddenly realized that he could change his life by himself and did not need to be dependent on others to help him or take care of him. Before this insight, he felt like he was just floating along without much control over his experiences, but now he believes that he has the ability to impact life events. He is able to establish and maintain schedules much better and has more control over his activities, what he does and when he does them. He is also aware that he has the ability to choose to make many parts of his life different.

In college and even as recently as eight years ago, he was bombarded with random noise in his head, and had great difficulty reading or focusing on personal goals. Medication and music helped, but sometimes he still became overwhelmed. Now he says, "I am almost back to normal, before I broke. The difference between then and now is that I still have a running commentary telling me what to say... but this commentary is something I don't want to get rid of." This present commentary may be the self-talk that everyone experiences but with an additional visual component, something like a teleprompter. He does not want to lose this because he finds it helpful as a guide or backup if he feels at a loss for words.

He added, "I am as normal as I want to be," which was music to my ears. He told me this as we sat on our deck outside on a warm summer day, and he looked contented, tuned in and motivated to enjoy our conversation and to enjoy his life. He has become the person that he wants to be, and that is the goal that we all have for our lives.

Many psychiatrists view the recovery from schizophrenia like that from diabetes. The disease is always there, but the symptoms that get in the way of living a relatively normal life can be controlled for many individuals (Torrey, 2019). In contrast, there is a growing body of research and experience that supports full recovery. This is a major paradigm shift in the treatment of schizophrenia.

In the mid-1990s, Courtenay Harding, PhD, reviewed and published worldwide studies that indicated that the recovery rate from schizophrenia ranged from 46 to 84 percent (Clay, 2014). These numbers indicated full recovery as well as only symptom improvement. Other research supports the idea that each decade following initial diagnosis increases the chances of recovery or improvement (Namade & Dombeck, 2009). The American Psychological Association training guidelines now incorporate a recovery orientation. Who would have thought this to be the case when I was in graduate school 40 years ago, or even 20 years ago when Jacob was first diagnosed? And how hopeful this must be for those newly diagnosed with schizophrenia.

In the end, I know that there are still many individuals with schizophrenia who will struggle with and without treatment. I also know that Jacob may or may not be one of the lucky ones to be completely symptom-free. Whether he does completely recover or learns to successfully cope with lingering symptoms, he has made amazing strides in his recovery process.

According to the Recovery to Practice program guidelines (APA & Jansen, 2014), he has met recovery goals: personal health, a stable home, a sense of purpose, and community participation and support. He has good health, eats well and occasionally exercises. He is a homeowner and lives in a supportive family environment. At this point his sense of purpose is to provide technical support to customers and financial and emotional support for his wife and brother-in-law. As for community support, he has friends that he enjoys and is active politically via social media. He has exceeded any expectations that I had based on my own antiquated training. This is what evolution is all about.

CHAPTER 10

FAMILY IMPACT OF SCHIZOPHRENIA

Schizophrenia has permeated and changed the relationships within our family in both positive and negative ways. On the positive side, my husband, daughter and I have admired how Jacob has developed coping skills and managed his symptoms. His ability to move forward is inspiring. My denial and perseverance kept me from thinking that his illness was insurmountable, and he seems to have this same perseverance, which drives him toward recovery and independence without the denial I felt. Most likely he struggles with this desire to live like his high school and college peers. Knowing that process is different for him must engender anger and frustration, and yet he does not seem to give up hope for his future.

On the negative side, he would direct his anger about his illness at me in many ways during the early years after his diagnosis. He went through a period when he blamed me for "making him" major in history when he was in college. After he graduated, it was hard for him to find a job, so I became the scapegoat. I did not force him to major in any subject and tried to support him when he made that choice himself. Neither of us could foresee the employment challenge experienced by history graduates, nor did we know that he would not want to follow the typical path of history majors, such as teaching, doing research or going to graduate school. He also directed his anger toward me at other times, such as when I would not let him and his wife move in with us or provide him with as much money as they wanted. To me these outbursts appeared to be projections of his anger at himself or displacement of his feelings because of the limitations of his illness. Either way it was easier to be mad at me and stop talking to me for a period of time rather than seeing the reality of his situation. Even though I felt deeply hurt when he cut me off, it was something that we both had to experience as part of the grieving and growth process. As hard as it was, we both had to realize that life was not going to be easy for Jacob. Part of his recovery meant that we had to accept these challenges before we could find a solution.

We have battled a lot about money over the years. "How much help did he need?" and "How much could I afford to help?" were the battle lines. He and his wife have often lived on the edge financially, meaning they do not have savings to cover unexpected expenses. They were routinely past due on their bills. It is true that many young people, even college graduates, have faced a challenging economy. A recent poll indicated that 40 percent of families in the US do not have $400 for emergency spending (Board of Governors of the Federal Reserve System, 2019.) Savings can be hard for many, but his illness most likely intensified the struggle. Over the years, he has run out of money before payday, experienced months of unemployment, had car accidents or car breakdowns, etc. The problem for me was that my finances were finite. Even before I retired, I could not afford to support them, nor did it seem like the right thing to do. I was never sure whether they would need to live with us or find some form of government support. Based on past results of his disability applications, getting such aid might not be so easy.

I knew that I couldn't in good conscience let him drive without insurance or allow his car to be repossessed since it was his only transportation to work. In his quest for independence, we have had many arguments about what is essential and what is something that you can live without. Teaching that balance is what most parents have to do. It is just more complicated when you aren't sure what your child is capable of doing. If he were "normal", letting him struggle and learn the hard way would be the tough but prudent choice. My dilemma was: how capable was he? Would he swim or would he get overwhelmed, give up and drown? Trying to mediate his real needs and his abilities has been a conundrum.

Looking back, I can truly say that every year gets better and better. His financial status is tenuous, but much improved, and he is making more realistic spending choices. We seldom argue about money now, and he never asks for help now unless he is truly in need. Also, he is more capable of paying me back if he needs a loan. Such a relief!

The other side of the relationship equation is the extended dependence that developed due to his illness. First, as a mother with a child who had ADHD. I made it my responsibility to structure Jacob's school-related activities more than I would have if he had not had the condition. Organizing his assignments and focusing on school-related tasks was a struggle for him. He seemed to need me to help him stay on track during homework and study time. That was often an exhausting and frustrating role. I would love to have relinquished it, but the extra structure enabled him to keep up academically. It was a trying period that we both hoped was time-limited. That being said, we already had a history of more mother involvement than most parent-child relationships by the time he developed schizophrenia.

Even without these added dynamics, Jacob and I have always been close, at least in my opinion. Since he was my firstborn and I only worked minimally during his early years, we spent a lot of time together. As he got older, our relationship was fairly open. We could talk about girlfriends, books, friends, politics, religion – whatever. Typical of many preteens and early teens, he also had private areas of his life that he kept from me. Like many parents, I found out these secret areas later. For example, I thought I was being pretty clever when I used his video game controllers as a form of discipline. When he needed a consequence for misbehaving and I had to go to work, I would take the game controllers with me. Much to my astonishment, after he moved out, I found a large popcorn canister of controllers in our basement that he had stashed as backups! He obviously didn't share everything.

During the first years of his illness, his dependence on me grew and he became even more open. At that time, he seemed to have

fewer filters on what he would tell me. In some ways that openness
was reassuring. I was able to understand what bothered him and
what parts of his life were going well. I knew if he was faring well at
school. He would tell me about friendships and some of the feelings
or behaviors around relationships that were confusing. At that time,
I was one of his main confidantes.

As he matured and created a bond with his wife, he became more
careful about what he shared. At the beginning of their marriage,
Rachel used to get very upset about how much he would share with
me about their relationship. I totally understand how she must have
felt. They seem to have worked that out, and actually, now the reverse
is true. He tells her everything that I say! Overall, Jacob is just more
candid than most people and less worried about how others might
see him. His approach reflects a lot of confidence and trust in other
people. Most of the time that works for him. At times, though, it most
likely makes him vulnerable.

Jacob might describe our relationship somewhat differently.
Although he appeared to share and, later, over-share during the
throes of his illness, he usually had difficulty telling me things that
he thought would anger or disappoint me. As previously mentioned,
assertiveness was an issue that he and his first psychologist addressed.
For instance, when he was in about seventh or eighth grade, he would
have about an hour between the time he got home from school and
the time I would get back from my office. On Wednesdays, he was
supposed come home, eat a snack and walk to his piano lesson,
which was only a couple blocks away. One Wednesday I got a call at
work from his piano teacher asking, "Is Jacob sick? He didn't show
up for his lesson." After I rushed home, I spotted him in the living
room intently engaged with a video game. Before telling him that his
teacher called me, I coolly asked him, "How was your piano lesson?"
Without taking his eyes off the game, he replied, "It was fine." When
I told him that he was busted, he added, "I thought I went." He
thought he went? Really? It would have been nice if he could have
said, "I didn't want to go today" or something a little more direct.

As close as we are, our relationship has also been characterized
by provocations on his part and over-reactions on mine. When he

was younger, he had a way of baiting me and I had to work at not reacting at hysterical levels. One afternoon when he was about five or six, we went to large mall in the Cincinnati area near our home. He evidently became bored and decided to spice up the shopping experience. He found the perfect hiding place in the middle of a rack of long dresses in the women's department. He was standing next to me one minute and – *bam!* – he was gone the next. Every parent's nightmare! Of course, I became frantic and enlisted other shoppers and store personnel to help search the entire building. Doors were covered by store security to make sure he or his potential kidnappers couldn't leave. After about 20 or 30 minutes, which seemed like hours, he popped out of his hiding place. He most likely achieved his goal that day.

Another memorable but more humorous provocation occurred grocery shopping with him when he was about seven years old. In those days produce was packed with ice in the display bins to keep it fresh, and he would love to eat the ice. Since I did not want him to eat it, one day I tried to use good parenting skills by setting the stage prior to entering the store. I very emphatically stated, "Jacob, please do not eat the ice around the vegetables today. The ice is needed for keeping the vegetables from spoiling and it may not even be clean for you to eat it. Make sure that you keep your hands in your pockets or behind your back while we are shopping today." So much for my calm preparations! Soon after, I found Jacob in the produce section of the store leaning over the ice and licking it. Of course, his hands were clasped behind his back! He could definitely be a defiant child.

Over the years, I learned that underreacting to provocations usually worked much better. I am definitely not perfect. It's still a challenge for me to say, "Oh how wonderful that you have rescued a third cat" when he has just borrowed money for his own food. Yet I try to remember that he and his wife are excellent caretakers of their pets, and their animals provide much joy. I also realize, of course, that when I am more composed, Jacob can be more open with me. My reactions are a work in progress. When I am calmer, I can encourage his assertiveness. To be sure, this has helped his stress levels and mine.

For many years I was in a state of constant worry about Jacob. When he acted so depressed in high school, suicide was a real worry. Being a psychologist and being aware that statistics are high for teen suicide, my responses to him and to his behaviors could be described as both vigilant and anxious. I certainly regret my actions during the high school band trip to California when I pounded on his hotel room door to see if he was okay. The intrusion was very upsetting to him but it was a very scary time. I had very little trust that he would be all right. Having a window into the future would have been extremely helpful. Knowing that his symptoms would eventually improve would have certainly reduced my internal trauma at the time.

This distrust and worry about suicide increased greatly after he was diagnosed with schizophrenia. Thirty percent of individuals who are diagnosed with this condition attempt suicide and one out of ten are successful (Center for Disease Control, 2017). Two of the most vulnerable times are when a person is younger and when they are newly diagnosed prior to treatment stabilization. Since Jacob was never hospitalized, I took on the huge weight of trying to protect him and to make sure that he was not entertaining thoughts of self-harm. One of his voices was very destructive and would disparage him constantly. This was the voice that would tell him to do things that would kill him. Jacob struggled mightily with this voice and to date has never engaged in self-destructive behavior except to sleep too much. But how was I to know? Looking back, my overreaction to his needs and my constant worry was understandable. This is a painful time to recall and it lasted for many years. As a mother I felt that I would do anything to try to protect him. So much of that period felt like a constant state of crisis. Even when relying on stress management techniques that had calmed me in the past, my life felt like an emotional rollercoaster.

Who would have guessed that the best was yet to come? As Jacob's symptoms began to stabilize and he finally became strong enough emotionally to separate, I have been able to let go so much more. The launching period happened gradually after college, and moving in with Rachel and marrying a year later was a positive attachment change for him. He loves her and has a strong desire to care for her. They are both presently highly motivated to be independent because they know there is no other choice right now. Independence itself can be empowering, and it is gratifying to see how they are figuring out how to make daily choices work.

The process is not always smooth. It is still filled with misunderstandings and anger at times, and we have had long breaks of weeks or months with little or no contact, usually because things were not going well for him. Fortunately, during the last few years, we have become Facebook friends. When he hasn't contacted me for a long time, I often interpret that as a red flag and check on him. "Stalking" him on Facebook provides the opportunity to assess how he is doing. More recently, silent times have not meant that he is upset or angry anymore but rather that he is doing fine, just busy. Presently our relationship seems to be back in balance. We meet about once a month for family time and dinner, and we text or talk on the phone regularly, but not daily. We enjoy staying in touch. It has taken 20 long years since his initial diagnosis to get to this point.

Our relationship has taken on new dimensions in other areas as well. Jacob is a good resource for technology help, as he is much more knowledgeable about my computer and phone than I could ever hope to be. When I was working, he would come over to my office and rescue me from programs gone bad, computer viruses and security issues. It was a comfort to know something could usually be done to keep my electronics up to date and functioning correctly. He has been very patient with my limited knowledge of technology.

I also like to discuss politics and current events with him. He is always aware of what is happening in the world and has opinions that I respect. Usually, we think alike, but if not, I can learn a lot from his opinions. These conversations allow me to still sneak in questions about his work, how his studies for new certification are going and how much time he spends on video games. I consciously try to limit those invasions and focus on keeping our relationship at an adult-to-adult level, however, which has been liberating for both of us.

His relationship with his sister has also been altered by his illness. Siblings who have a brother or sister with mental illness often have mixed feelings. Lukens and associates (2004) interviewed individuals who had siblings with severe mental illness and gathered both the negative and positive effects of living with a family member who had such a diagnosis. Many reported sadness in the way the condition changed their brother or sister and grieved the loss of the former relationship that they once had. They also expressed anger at the negative changes to their sibling and their family structure and felt guilty that they survived the genetic transmission. They did believe, however, that their sibling's encounter with serious mental illness made them more compassionate towards others and less tolerant of stigma-associated behaviors. Of course, the interviewees strongly wished that their brother or sister could be well.

Elizabeth has always felt loyal and supportive toward Jacob. Like many older brothers, he liked to antagonize her and her friends at times, but I am sure it worked both ways. For the most part, however, they enjoyed playing together and sharing in family activities. I have fond memories of them racing their hamsters in homemade mazes, making look-outs in the woods behind our house and playing diving games at the lake when visiting Grandma and Grandpa. Elizabeth looked up to Jacob as her big brother and seemed to be proud to be his sister. When he became active in the high school band, she eventually became part of the color guard. When he decided to go to UC, she did the same, and they even lived in the same dorm during her first year.

Often, growing up in a family with one sibling having a special diagnosis like Jacob's ADHD or later schizophrenia could lead to the "healthy" sibling feeling resentful or left out. A parent's time and attention can easily be absorbed by the problems presented by a child with special needs. While Elizabeth was aware of Jacob's issues, she adamantly denies feeling pushed aside. Both were equally active in their extracurricular activities and both frequently entertained friends at our house. Elizabeth spent many hours with her best friend since kindergarten as well as other friends who lived nearby.

Jacob did the same. They were both involved in separate but equally time-demanding activities. Elizabeth was in a pre-professional dance program that required many hours of classes while Jacob took piano lessons and drum lessons, and was active in Boy Scouts and church youth groups. How we managed to balance everything during those eight or so years that I was a single parent seems like a miracle. It was actually a blur to me – working full-time and managing family meals, transportation to and from activities, and having consistent, positive family time. Fortunately, we have videos of some of those moments. To validate Elizabeth's claim that she felt equal and as cared about as her brother, these videos do show a remarkable balance of attention. Being aware of that issue of possible imbalance and being blessed with a lot of energy, I worked hard to give equal time to them both.

When Jacob was first diagnosed with schizophrenia, Elizabeth did not have a complete picture of all that Jacob was experiencing. Being only 15 at the time of his onset, she did not understand the full impact of his disease. His behavior was often confusing to her. Of course, she and I discussed his illness. We watched educational videos about schizophrenia and read information that increased her knowledge. But living with a brother who exhibits symptoms of severe mental illness is different than reading about it or seeing it from an adult perspective. She remembers that some of his habits were very irritating to her and, at the time, she felt he was purposefully trying to push her buttons. It was hard for her to sort through what was sibling harassment and what was behavior that he did not know how to control.

One memory she has was of a camping trip that we took to the Rocky Mountains. This was the summer following his diagnosis. Although Jacob had been in college for one year, he still exhibited behaviors that were hard to understand. Usually when we camped as a family, Elizabeth always ended up on the side of the tent that sloped and caught rain water. That is what happened that night. Because she couldn't sleep, she moved to the back seat of our van, where it was dry and quiet. The next morning, Jacob got up very early before the sun arose and began digging through the back of the van where the food was stored. He loudly opened and slammed closed the back hatch of the van over and over again. He stomped around the campsite making crunching sounds with his shoes on the twigs and rocks. Basically, he kept her from the rest she so wanted. At the time she thought he was intentionally trying to be a pain and she was furious at him. Looking back now, she attributes it to some agitation that he was most likely experiencing.

On that same trip, we visited the Garden of the Gods Visitor and Nature Center near Colorado Springs. This is a beautiful red rock park with at least 20 trails, and at the beginning of our walk, Jacob separated from Elizabeth and me. Wandering away from us was something that he often did when we traveled, but he always reconnected with us after a short time. We didn't worry about it too much at first and kept thinking that we would run into him soon. While walking the convoluted path around huge rock formations, we would look with expectant eyes as we turned a corner, or we would slow our pace in the hope that he was behind us. When we hadn't found him by the end of the route, my anxiety began to skyrocket. Finally, at dusk before the park closed, we had to enlist the help of the park police to help us. I can see how frustrated Elizabeth must have been because a part of me was angry as well. Mostly I was just frightened and extremely alarmed and I am sure she shared those fears too. When we finally reunited, he was quiet and said very little about where he went. I am sure it would be easy for Elizabeth to think he was trying to make life difficult for us like he did when he was younger. This experience had a completely different feeling to it, though. He did not exude any impish smiles or laughter afterwards. Instead, his eyes looked frightened and he acted very anxious and withdrawn for the rest of the evening.

Over the years, Elizabeth has developed a better understanding of Jacob's illness. Initially she and I watched Dr Fred Frese's DVD about his recovery process over and over again. My daughter learned as much as she could and tried to be supportive. Later, when she was in graduate school for occupational therapy, she developed a special interest in mental health treatment. One of her school projects included writing an educational flyer to explain serious mental illness to families whose loved ones may be entering treatment. This was a useful research project for her to put together so that others could understand more about schizophrenia. Writing the booklet was helpful to her as well because she had to do more personal research in order to compose it. Her work was helpful for clients in my practice too.

She would like to be closer to Jacob and see him more often. He was a groomsman in her wedding ten years ago, and he has interacted with her children at their respective homes and at family gatherings. Contact seems strained at times and Jacob's comfort level has varied according to how he is feeling. I do believe that they love each other and would be there for each other in a crisis. Both are now pursuing their own family goals and activities, which can be time-consuming. He is working two jobs to stay afloat, so he has very little free time. She works part-time as an occupational therapist and parents three active little girls. Hopefully, in the future, they will have even more intersections. Now that Jacob is trying to attend more family functions, these encounters appear to be increasing.

Of course, support from my husband Glen has been invaluable for Jacob as well. He already knew that he had signed on to parent two teenagers when he married me, so he expected some challenges. Overall, our initial family adjustments were minimal. Both kids enjoyed being with Glen, although they never let him pick out family movies! He was and still is a pilot, and they liked to go flying with him. We have had a lot of adventurous family vacations and camping trips, some of which included his children, spouses and grandchildren, too. Our extended family holidays are always fun and noisy, especially with 16 grandchildren now. Little did he or I suspect that we would be facing a serious mental illness two years into our marriage.

The learning curve was high for me after Jacob's diagnosis, but it was even higher for Glen. As an engineer, his educational background did not include many psychology classes. He met with Jacob's psychologist, however, and became an active team member to support Jacob through those early times. I relied on him to keep me focused and to give objective advice when we had big decisions to make. Those early years were incredibly stressful for us, but we trudged through most of the big issues on the same page.

After Jacob had his relapse and moved home, we began to see that his recovery process was going to be more complicated than we had originally thought. We decided that we needed more outside support and began to participate in the Family-to-Family program sponsored by the National Alliance on Mental Illness (NAMI). As a mental health professional, I knew much of the information about serious mental illness and possible relapses. Living with someone with a psychotic illness, however, was more challenging than reading case studies or seeing individuals for 45 minutes per week in my practice. In addition, my husband had many concerns and needed to understand the issues we were facing as a family. He and I had to be more unified in the ways we helped Jacob. Both of us were often impatient or tried different approaches at different times that divided our efforts and probably interfered with Jacob's progress. Our 12-week Family-to-Family course was a turning point in our ability to grasp the total picture and not be caught up in the details. It gave us the ability to make the transition from treading water to finally swimming in a forward motion again.

Our family help from NAMI rates as an invaluable experience. The Family-to-Family program was facilitated by volunteers, usually parents or relatives of someone with a serious mental health condition. Listening and sharing our stories with others whose loved ones were at various phases of illness and recovery was helpful and hopeful. The experience cut through our sense of isolation and validated what I knew about the healing aspects of group support.

Irvin D Yalom (1975), an early and well-known researcher in the field of group therapy, found that being with others who have similar experiences can be healing in and of itself. Glen and I often felt isolated, and we didn't have any friends with a son who was diagnosed with schizophrenia. Because the other participants and the Family-to-Family leaders were at different stages of coping with the illness, we learned how they were able to manage and felt more hopeful.

We came away from the group knowing that change for Jacob and for us was not only possible, but likely.

We also obtained valuable community resources. The group setup encouraged interaction among participants and allowed for us to give and receive assistance from them as well. During the initial meetings we were able to vent our frustrations and tell our story to people who could really understand. To avoid staying stuck in our frustration, we received good, updated information about the process of schizophrenia and reassurance that we did not have to feel guilty or responsible for creating the symptoms. We came away with a plan about how we were going to approach our challenges with Jacob.

One of the more interesting activities that we engaged in during our Family-to-Family program helped us to understand what it might be like to be Jacob, to have auditory hallucinations or voices that constantly bother you. We did this by dividing into triads with two people standing behind one person who was sitting in a chair. The seated person tried to read a passage of some kind while the two standing behind conversed with one another – like auditory hallucinations might be doing. To be sitting in the position of the person with the voices was very difficult. It was then that I got it. I understood why Jacob would withdraw or want to sleep, and how hard it was for him to study when his medications were not working or he was under stress. It is one thing to intellectually think about how he might feel but quite another to try to experience it even for a short time.

We also received a binder that we filled with handouts from each class, which included local resources as well as up-to-date research about various mental health diagnoses. This binder has been very helpful over the years, especially during the times that we hit a wall or needed reminders that what we were experiencing was "normal" or expected and that change usually takes time and effort.

With work and lots of talking and listening to each other, Glen and I have developed a more unified approach and found ways to respond to challenges more strategically and calmly. Even with newfound information, support and energy, the process of helping my son cope with his serious mental illness is still challenging, but not nearly as difficult as it used to be. Do we still flounder at times? Absolutely!

We still do not have all of the answers nor have we figured out everything that anyone facing schizophrenia needs to know. Having all of the answers may be an impossible goal, but having resources and coping skills to recover from challenges is achievable. Some of the obstacles are predictable and some are not. Having control over the disease or its consequences is not always possible, but having better control over our responses to the setbacks can help. Because of this and the healing of community experience, sharing stories with others in similar circumstances was very important for us.

Together we have spent many hours figuring out approaches to help Jacob finish college and, more importantly, to help him learn how to be happy and independent. Glen recognized Jacob's intellectual strengths and could better encourage independence. Not that I did not think that Jacob was smart, but I had more fears about his ability to be independent. We may have played the good cop-bad cop game, but we didn't always play the same roles. Sometimes Glen would be the tough one and would criticize me for being too lenient. When I would give Jacob extra money for a bill that was past due, he thought he would never learn to budget. On the other hand, when I would put a limit on the amount to help with car repairs, Glen would remind me that having a car is essential to working and being independent. Finding the middle ground to encourage financial stability has been tough, but having each other as a sounding board has been immensely important.

Schizophrenia is an individual diagnosis, but the illness impacts everyone who loves and cares for someone who suffers from it. None of us would have chosen this path for Jacob. Some would say it was the roll of the dice. However, we loved and still love him and do not want to abandon him. More than not deserting him, though, my husband, my daughter and I remain involved as part of his support team. Hopefully he experiences and understands how much we love and support him.

CHAPTER 11

FIGHTING STEREOTYPES

Fighting misconceptions about schizophrenia is an important way to support Jacob and all individuals with this illness. Unfortunately, stigma does not respond to psychotherapy or medication, and it continues to surround us and haunt us. From my own experience I have found certain people are open and understanding, some may just pretend to be accepting, and others just plain back away. The media does not always help either. It is important to me to be an advocate for anyone with mental illness, including my son. Being more forthright and embracing opportunities to educate people about his illness can prevent the perpetuation of myths and misunderstandings.

That being said, opening up with other people about Jacob's diagnosis produced a mixed bag of responses. I quickly learned not to share this information everywhere I went. To begin with, it was my son's diagnosis to share. Most likely my goal in sharing initially was to look for support either for him or for myself. We needed resources and emotional support. I felt confused, sad and in need of hugs. Now the sharing is more often to clear up misconceptions about schizophrenia.

As soon as he was diagnosed and started medication, I met with his high school teachers in a team meeting. Because he already had an academic accommodation plan due to his ADHD, I had met with some of the teachers earlier in the school year on an individual basis. Now we sat in a conference room around a large table while they listened attentively to the difficulties associated with his new diagnosis.

Since he would sometimes sleep in class due to medication side effects, it was important that they were on board. All of the teachers expressed concern and offered support. They were willing to have him continue in their classes and provide him extra accommodations if needed. Every one of the teachers was helpful. They all discussed ways to reduce stress for him in their classroom. At one point, his science teacher commented that Jacob must be very smart to have coped with symptoms of schizophrenia and still perform as well as he did at school. That was music to my ears! This was one of the first times I shared his diagnosis with anyone outside of family, and their responses were so encouraging. The best part, of course, was that Jacob benefited from this early experience with open-minded professionals.

Another example early on was not so supportive. At church after a Sunday service, I was noticeably upset. Something had triggered a sad memory or perhaps I was feeling down seeing all of Jacob's friends enjoying themselves while he was at home still fighting his debilitating voices. One of the parishioners I had known for quite a long while asked why I looked so sad. When I shared my story about Jacob's illness, I received a polite response: "Oh, I am sorry to hear that." That was all she said and then she found an excuse to walk away. I also told a few other people at our church who I thought would be helpful and received similar coldness. I felt devastated and confused. This was a church that my children and I had been actively a part of for 13 years. Jacob had been on three mission trips, was an acolyte for many years, confirmed in the church as an early teen, and was active with the youth program, small as it was. I am not writing this to accuse the people in this parish as being cold and unfeeling, but because it was then that I realized what a stigma his mental illness was going to be. As a psychologist it was certainly easier for me to make the leap of parity, but many other people still had fears and misunderstandings about mental illness.

About the time Jacob started college, I reconnected with a friend who was a psychologist, too. I was in my hurting, vulnerable, open mode and again blurted out how worried I was about my son and his illness. Shockingly enough, she said she totally understood because her older sister also had schizophrenia. We spent a long time talking that afternoon and continued to develop a very close friendship over the years. She was very helpful, compassionate and always there to help me sort through the challenges. Openness paid off that time.

Another good friend recently reminded me of a time, near the onset of his diagnosis, that I decided to share Jacob's illness. We were with a group of psychologists who had been friends for many years, and she remembers being appalled at their reactions. Instead of being sympathetic, they went into fix-it mode. Almost all of them insisted that I needed to help him apply for Social Security Disability. I was resisting and saying that we were not ready for that. Looking back, they were absolutely right – I really wish that I had. At that time his symptoms were more active, so he probably would have qualified for more help without too much difficulty. I was not, however, ready to see him as disabled. Their intentions were good and their advice was spot-on, but I was not there yet, and really what I needed from them was their understanding.

I was still experiencing denial that his illness could possibly last a lifetime, and maybe that denial was a reflection of my own stigmatizing. Previously, I had worked for the State of Ohio administering tests to determine if someone with a disability qualified for government support. Being determined not to categorize Jacob as disabled at the time is a reflection of my own denial and bias that his illness was not that serious.

There is another component to the disability aid related to self-stigma. While many people truly need and benefit from government assistance, for some individuals the aid can be a trap that impairs improvement. Getting disability benefits at the beginning of an illness, when the possibility of recovery or remission is unknown, may interfere with someone's motivation to improve. I have seen that in my practice and have been reluctant to support an application if I thought the client could eventually recover and be self-supporting. Other psychologists have also experienced this. Once a person has received disability aid for a mental illness, that becomes a financial safety net that is hard to abandon. Consequently, symptoms may not improve for fear of losing disability payments. This does not necessarily mean that someone is scamming the system, although that occasionally happens. It's more that they are fearful that they cannot live without help, thinking, *What if I cannot manage? What happens if I lose my job?* While you can still get disability at a reduced rate if you are working and not making above a certain amount of money, many may work but underachieve so as not to lose that additional income. Plus, getting government assistance may negatively impact self-esteem and self-empowerment. Applying for disability at a later time, after all recovery attempts have been unsuccessful, has advantages. Perhaps my reluctance early on benefited Jacob in the long run.

Jacob felt the same confusion about self-disclosure – who to tell, when to tell them, and who not to tell at all. At college he had his group of friends through the Disability Office. He could be completely open with them and he found that very supportive. Otherwise, he had devised a rule only to discuss his illness when asked. So, if someone saw him taking medication and became curious, he would explain why. Later, as social media grew with Myspace, then Facebook, he became very open on these platforms. At first, he used schizophrenia as part of his profile or self-description. This may have been a problem later for employment, as social media posts can usually negatively impact a job search for anyone who is too honest about themselves. At this point in time, he says that he is generally much less open on Facebook. He probably learned the hard way, but there is no way to prove it.

After my initial experiences of sharing, I also tried to pick and choose who I talked to about his schizophrenic symptoms. We found another church that had many supportive and understanding parishioners. Participating in NAMI activities was another good outlet for sharing candidly with others. I also have several very good friends who I can comfortably talk to about our experiences without feeling judged or inducing panic.

The friend whose sister developed schizophrenia during her college years continued to be a great source of understanding. She too tried to help me think about the reality of applying for disability aid. She also understood how hard it was to carry the emotional burden of worrying about a loved one with schizophrenia. She allowed me to explore my feelings and experiences without judgment. Another friend was also very supportive. She was always there to help me sort through issues, vent my frustration and come up with a solution to manage whatever challenge we were facing, and she very kindly gave Jacob an iPod while he was in college to help him reduce the distractions from his voices. One of my best friends from high school was also very comforting. She sent me a heart pin to wear as a token of her support. It is still a great reminder and she is still a great friend. Having a compassionate inner circle certainly helps to counteract the worry about stigma and judgment.

As time went on, I felt less frazzled and more clear-headed about what Jacob was experiencing so it was easier to take greater risks. This meant talking about my son's illness with other people who might not be so accepting. I wanted others to see schizophrenia like any other illness. The risk of misunderstanding has been worth it. It wasn't about me or my feelings anymore. It became a personal mission about making life easier for those who experience mental illness. My goal was to find ways to educate and break down stigmas so others wouldn't be afraid of Jacob, react to him in prejudicial ways, or even do or say something harmful to him. While it was my son's story to tell, if I didn't share as well when opportunities arose, then I would be guilty of perpetuating the stigma and misunderstanding of schizophrenia. Looking the other way allows bias to continue.

How did I begin to do this? Looking at what the media was broadcasting was a starter. There are always plenty of opinions floating around about mental illness in general, but especially mental illness with a psychotic component. In addition, I needed to really listen to other people to discover the biases that existed and why some people would back away from talking about schizophrenia. A 2006 study indicated that stigma against people with schizophrenia had actually increased over a ten-year period. More respondents said that they were unwilling to have someone with schizophrenia as their neighbor in comparison to a survey taken in 1996. The majority of the public in the more recent study did not want to work or socialize with someone with schizophrenia, or have someone in their family marry someone with schizophrenia (Pescosolido, 2010). I wanted to understand why such a bias existed for them and why social acceptance was decreasing.

I also had to make sure my knowledge of the facts and research were up to date and accurate so I could confront misinformation. Fortunately, good research is not hard to find now. Because of better medications and treatment, more people with schizophrenia are able to lead productive lives outside of hospitals. Behavioral scientists are studying the new generation of people with schizophrenia. The new studies are producing results that help to shed light on a diagnosis that used to be seen as hopeless.

Beginning with stories on the nightly news, it was easy to guess that many people associate schizophrenia with the rising rate of mass murders. One of the most fear-invoking misunderstandings about schizophrenia is the idea that a person with schizophrenia is unpredictable and dangerous. A Gallup poll in 2019 revealed that 83 per cent of Americans blamed an inadequate mental health system for mass shootings that have occurred in our country (Saad, 2019). An earlier survey in 2013 found that 46 percent of the people in the US thought people with mental illness were more dangerous than the general population. When looking at surveys about schizophrenia in particular, 60 percent of Americans thought that people diagnosed with schizophrenia were "likely" to "very likely" to commit a violent act (Potts, 2014).

These fears are perpetuated by the media. McGinty et al. (2016) studied trends in news coverage in the US, and their analysis of 400 articles between 1995 and 2014 indicated that the media associates violence with mental illness, most especially schizophrenia, out of proportion to actual rates. In the second decade of the years studied, these stories tended to be on the front page. This kind of coverage can be influential in creating and perpetuating the fear of those diagnosed with schizophrenia.

In contrast to public opinion, research findings indicate that people with mental illness have a risk factor of being violent on par with the general population. Mental illness includes psychotic disorders, substance abuse and personality disorders. Although Swanson's work supports a low rate for all mental illness, psychotic disorders such as schizophrenia and bipolar disorder have the lowest rates. In reality, mental illness is a poor predictor of violence. According to Jeffrey Swanson and Allison G Robertson in their article "Thinking Differently about Mental Illness, Violence Risk, and Gun Rights" (2015), violence in the US would only be reduced by 4 percent if in the future we could cure all mental illness.

While there are certainly some people with serious mental illness who become violent, they make up a small percentage. Recent attempts to profile mass shooters have produced inconsistent results. More often a complex interaction of psychological, social, economic and cultural factors underlie motivations for violent shootings (Metz. & MacLeish, 2015). While two-thirds of the mass shooters do have a history of mental health issues, that is only somewhat higher than the general population, given 50 percent of the general population will have a diagnosis of mental illness at some time in their life. According to The Violence Project's research, mental illness was partly responsible for violence in only 15.8 percent of mass shootings. While the percentage is high, that still means that 84 percent of the shootings happen for other reasons. Researchers Jillian K Peterson and James A Densley of The Violence Project continue to search for reasons and patterns. Childhood trauma, crises and personal grievances, an inspiration or validation for their belief, and access to guns are all factors that outweigh possible psychotic motivations (Peterson & Densley, 2019).

Swanson and his associates (2015) found that there are times when individuals with serious mental illness are at risk of harming themselves or others, such as when they are initially released from a hospitalization. They suggest that these are times when guns should be restricted, at least temporarily. The majority of people with serious mental illness, however, are non-violent people who never cause problems of this sort, even post-hospitalization. Nevertheless, the stigma still exists.

In fact, violence to others is not a characteristic of most people with serious mental illness. According to an article published in the *American Journal of Public Health* (Desmarais et al., 2014), most individuals with severe mental illness, particularly schizophrenia, are more at risk of harming themselves than others and are more often the *victims* of crime or abuse because of their social vulnerability. They are usually passive and unguarded, not violent and dangerous. According to Nestor's study (2002), in general, individuals with schizophrenia actually become less violent over time because they tend to withdraw and socially isolate themselves. Because of the passivity and disordered thinking associated with schizophrenia, these individuals are 65–130 percent more likely to be victims of violence than other members of the general population.

Those are the facts that need to be inserted in my discussions with others, as it is important that people know that my son is not dangerous. He and many others with a similar diagnosis should be able to seek treatment and services that they need without fear of being labeled by others as psychotic murderers. With the increases in violence and mass killings, it is more important than ever for the real facts about mental illness to be heard. Being able to talk about mental illness without stigmatizing the person or the family will lead to more successful treatment and more people willing to seek treatment.

If Jacob had not grown up in a psychologically oriented family, perhaps he would have been reluctant to seek help. Many individuals try to ignore or fight their diagnosis or symptoms. In their article about the stigma of mental illness, Shrivastava, Johnston and Bureau (2012) explain that stigma can prevent individuals with mental illness from seeking treatment. They say stigma may also impede continuity of care or medication compliance. For psychotic individuals especially, this delay may lead to more profound neurocognitive disturbances and possibly increase violence to others or to self. In these cases, stigma can produce stigma. This complicates how open to be with other people, and at the same time points to how important it is to educate others.

For instance, when Jacob is interviewing for jobs, should he tell his employer that he has schizophrenia? Legally, his illness falls under the protection of the Americans with Disabilities Act. He is entitled to accommodations and employers are not allowed to discriminate either in hiring or firing him based on his illness. In the real world, though, stigmas still play a strong part in employer-employee relationships in many work organizations. No matter how open-minded an employer may be, once an illness is disclosed, it does have an impact. It's like telling a person, "Try not to see anything in the room that might be the color blue." Of course, they will suddenly be conscious of all the blue items around them. It isn't that most people want to be biased, but mental illness, especially schizophrenia, is still often misunderstood.

Jacob does not share his diagnosis during a job interview, just as most people do not share their illnesses in the same scenario. If you have diabetes or irritable bowel syndrome, do you talk about that in a job interview? Probably not! Instead, he tells his supervisors later, if and when he needs accommodations. Does that affect his job promotions? That is difficult to know and hard to prove, but Jacob does not think that it has for him. Some people with schizophrenia will tell employers that they are taking medication to help with anxiety rather than give the employer the name of their diagnosis. It is true that antipsychotic medication helps with anxiety and omitting the diagnosis may help to avoid stigma. At the same time, hiding mental illness will never lead others to understand, accept or be comfortable with the idea that someone with such a diagnosis can be a valuable employee.

While he did lose his job after posting the article about a nearby mass murder on the employee website, Jacob is sure that he was fired for breaking a strict company rule about what information he was allowed to share there. He was also very agitated by the new medication that he was taking. I still wonder, however, if his openness about his diagnosis at that job made others more wary. Even though he only wanted to inform others who lived in the community, his post may have seemed threatening to those who knew his diagnosis.

While harming others is not a typical behavior of schizophrenia, the risk of self-harm is not a myth. In an article entitled "Outcomes and Recovery Factors of Schizophrenia", Nemade and Dombeck (2009) report that during the first ten years of experiencing schizophrenia, about 10 percent of patients commit suicide and the percentage increases to 15 percent during the next 20 years. The reasons may be varied, but most likely center around uncontrolled auditory and visual hallucinations as well as disordered thinking. It was very anxiety-provoking and scary for my son to hear things that he had no control over. The voices were incessant prior to medication. Also, he knew that his illness could be life-changing and long-lasting. How could he not have felt hopeless and depressed? Fortunately, at the time he had resources for good psychological counseling to cope with these issues. Not everyone makes it through those periods of highest risk or recovers as well as Jacob has, however.

Another period of high suicide risk is after being released from inpatient hospitalization (Siris, 2001). Most hospitalizations are much briefer than in the past, usually one to two weeks at the most, and the focus is to evaluate and stabilize medications and to provide short-term psychological interventions. It is important that a person who is at high risk for suicide continue to engage in psychological counseling once they are back in the community. Finding coping strategies, developing insight and validating personal strengths through therapy can be an important part of the recovery process. Many good psychiatric hospitals now make sure that patients have an appointment with a psychologist or counselor prior to release from the hospital.

Besides the fear of violence, literature in the field of schizophrenia reports other misconceptions about the condition. Some of the myths include the belief that individuals with schizophrenia can never recover or lead a productive life, that most will have to be institutionalized or jailed, and that someone else will always have to make treatment decisions for them. These beliefs are leftovers from pre-antipsychotic medication days. In the past, when medications did not help with active symptom reduction, oftentimes institutionalization was the only answer for the safety of the patient. And although there are varying degrees of recovery and varying degrees of recovery rates even now, most individuals with a diagnosis of schizophrenia are able to work, manage their finances, and live independently in a manner that was unheard of 50 or 60 years ago.

Jacob is a prime example. The good news is that within ten years of initial treatment, 50 percent of individuals with schizophrenia are either completely recovered or improved to the point of being able to function independently. With treatment, the percentage continues to increase (Namade & Dombeck, 2009).

Dr Frese recalls an experience of stigma associated with recovery early in his treatment. He was diagnosed with paranoid schizophrenia at age 25 and spent several months in a psychiatric hospital at the time. One of the young, and evidently inexperienced, psychologists told him, "If it weren't for your illness, you could become a professional." This is an example of how even mental health experts can stigmatize by sending the message that you will probably never be able to recover (Kersting, 2005).

Of course, recovery varies. Again, we are looking at statistics, and not everyone fits a statistical pattern. Presently a small percentage of people with schizophrenia do not improve or they refuse help. Surveys of the homeless population indicate that at least 25 percent have a severe mental illness (National Coalition for the Homeless, 2017). As a society we need a way to reach out and help those individuals. Identifying new strategies could include more available housing, community resources and intervention programs. Yes, some of these services do exist, but obviously not enough. Families who have relatives who fall through the cracks need significant support as well.

Although I have never encountered this belief, according to an article in *Memory & Cognition* (Marsh & Shanks, 2014), some people think schizophrenia is contagious. While it is true that schizophrenia is often genetically transmitted, even that transmission is not 100 percent. The occurrence of the condition for children of a parent with schizophrenia is ten times greater than the general population. If someone with schizophrenia has an identical twin, the other twin has a 48 percent chance of developing it, and the percentages decrease rapidly the more distant the relative with the illness. If an adult has schizophrenia, their child has a 17 percent chance of developing the illness, their sibling a 9 percent chance, and any second-degree relative a 4 percent chance. Note that the chance of someone in the general population developing schizophrenia is 1 percent (Gottesman, 1991). Perhaps the idea of contagiousness is related to the observance of some parents with schizophrenia producing a child or children with this illness. More likely, though, it is fear and lack of education that may perpetuate the myth that "you better stay away from someone with schizophrenia because after a period of time you too might catch it."

Friends ask me if having schizophrenia means that Jacob has a split personality. Does he have the "Dr Jekyll and Mr Hyde" syndrome? Without any warning, will he become aggressive or psychopathic? The answer is a capital N-O. While it is true that the word schizophrenia actually means "split mind", from the Greek words *skhizein* ("split") and *phren* ("mind"), this illness was named before the symptoms of schizophrenia were understood. Diagnostically, symptoms of split personality or multiple personality exist under the category of dissociative disorders (American Psychiatric Association, 2013). Dissociative disorders are very different from schizophrenia. Individuals with a dissociative disorder exhibit varying degrees of autonomous personality states that, until treatment, they do not even know exist. They may act in completely different ways depending on which one is active at the time, and often dissociative disorders develop as a method of coping with severe trauma or abuse. Whereas schizophrenia is genetic, dissociative disorders are not. Individuals with dissociative disorders typically do not have thought disorders, hallucinations or any of the other positive or negative symptoms of schizophrenia. So, no, Jacob will not display multiple parts of himself.

The other major myth, one that dominated my early struggles for understanding, is that schizophrenia is caused by someone's social or family experiences. Twin adoption studies during the late 1970s traced genetic indicators and found that schizophrenia is associated with biology, not the home environment or caregiver's behavior (Kety, Rosenthal & Wender, 1978). I cannot emphasize enough that schizophrenia is a brain disease with genetic correlations. Yes, stress can be associated with its manifestation, but it may simply be related to the ordinary strain of human development. Fortunately, we can dispel the idea that schizophrenia is caused by other outside forces, such as witchcraft, evil spirits or demons. We have modern science to thank for more accurate thinking.

Sometimes, people associate "madness" with "brilliance". Science has yet to prove that people with high intellectual functioning are any more likely to develop schizophrenia. Yes, there are exceptional individuals like John Nash, who was both brilliant and had schizophrenia, though he was an extraordinary person in general and not necessarily a reflection of all people with the same condition. That being said, there is a subset of individuals with higher-than-average IQs that have schizophrenia. According to Cernis et al. (2015), while individuals with this illness who have high IQs do experience positive symptoms such as hallucinations and thought disorder, they tend to have higher global functioning, are more emotionally expressive, have better insight and have fewer negative symptoms and disorganization than most individuals with similar diagnoses. Their intellectual functioning may make it easier to cope with symptoms or, as the authors suggest, their condition may actually be a separate type of schizophrenia. Whatever the reason, these individuals tend to recover more fully and have fewer leftover symptoms to accommodate. It is possible that Jacob's intelligence is one of the factors that has contributed to his improvement.

My husband says that when he was growing up, he thought people with schizophrenia had lower IQs. Of course, he knows that is not true of Jacob. Is this another myth associated with such a diagnosis? People with schizophrenia most likely span the same bell-shaped curve of intelligence that illustrates the IQ of the general population. In general, most people fall in the middle and the higher and lower extremes extend toward the sides of the curve. Some research indicates that many people with schizophrenia fall toward lower-than-average functioning (Russell, 1997). The problem assessing the IQs of people with schizophrenia is very complicated, however, because scores are based on a total range of intellectual functioning. Therefore, lower scores would be expected for people struggling with a thought disorder, decreased visual motor speed and memory impairment. Scores on subtests assessing these areas of functioning can decrease a person's overall score. Even depression, anxiety and untreated ADHD can make for a seemingly lower IQ. The problem in these cases may have to do with the assessment method, not the illness. Based on these complications, the research on intelligence and schizophrenia is too complex to make any generalizations.

The good news is that pharmaceutical progress may be a game-changer for some people with schizophrenia. The areas of intellectual functioning often impaired by this condition can change at least to a moderate degree and may shine a different light on the earlier research. Studies have shown that newer atypical antipsychotic medications can correct neurocognitive disturbances. These changes can improve the executive functioning, inattention and verbal memory problems associated with schizophrenia, and although all medications have side effects, individuals who find that newer formulations work for them may be able to improve their quality of life (Sumiyoshi et al., 2014).

At this point in time, my son still qualifies for medical insurance as part of the Affordable Care Act. His mental health services are paid on par with his physical health services. It is so important to have mental and physical illness parity, not only in regard to insurance reimbursement but in the social realm as well. Eliminating the fears and misunderstanding associated with schizophrenia will also break down the barriers to seeking treatment and, as a result, can improve recovery. This would also make life easier for those with schizophrenia to find employment and enjoy more social acceptance.

Movies such as *A Beautiful Mind* and *The Soloist* have helped to promote understanding of how schizophrenia can be painful to the afflicted and their loved ones. They help to break down some of the embarrassment associated with mental illness. Our society goes through phases of shame and secrecy about various illnesses. For example, when my great-grandparents' son had tuberculosis, the word was whispered and the diagnosis hidden. The stigma at that time was fear of contagion and lack of understanding. In my grandparents' era and early in my parents' generation, cancer was the disease that everyone talked about in a hushed voice. Both illnesses were to be feared because treatments were not very successful during their generations, whereas people discuss these diagnoses openly nowadays, and programs about cancer and ads for treatment are often aired on television. Public acceptance of mental illness is growing as well, but there is still much misunderstanding. We see ads for treatment of depression and anxiety, but many biases still exist about psychotic conditions such as schizophrenia.

My vision of the perfect world is that we are all open and understanding without prejudice and judgement toward those who are different from us. Inclusion supersedes otherness. It is thinking about some people as other that stirs fear and misunderstandings. Complete acceptance may still be a fantasy, but it can be used as a guide. We can all do our part to make the path easier for those with serious mental illness. Dispelling myths is one of the big reasons I wanted to write this book. It is important for Jacob, for myself and for all who read this book to take advantage of these teaching moments.

Here are three easy, yet courageous, steps that we can all take:

1. Be an educator.

When friends or family make negative references about individuals with schizophrenia, share facts. The National Alliance on Mental Illness (www.nami.org), the National Institute of Mental Health (www.nimh.nih.gov), or Schizophrenia.com websites provide useful, up-to-date information. Politely confront misinformation.

2. Be respectful.

Words can be powerful. A study in Britain found hundreds of derogatory words used to describe people with mental illness (Rose et al., 2007). Making fun of someone who has hallucinations or unusual beliefs because of a mental illness is hurtful to them and to people who care about them. Few people joke about cancer or diabetes.

Respect also includes using the term "schizophrenic" as an adjective for a behavior or symptoms, not as a noun for a person who has schizophrenia. Someone diagnosed with schizophrenia is just that: someone who has the disease. They are not the disease itself – i.e., a schizophrenic. Again, using a physical health analogy, a person who has arrhythmia or irregular heartbeats is not called an arrhythmic.

3. Be compassionate.

Those who suffer from schizophrenia need support and understanding. Even if they display unusual behaviors, they are unlikely to be harmful. Untreated symptoms or relapses in treatment may be frightening to them. The times when their thoughts are confused and behaviors are strange may be when they need the most kindness. Empathy can make a difference.

CHAPTER 12

ESSENTIALS OF SELF-CARE

What airline passenger truly loves flying in turbulent conditions? The seatbelt signs begin to glow, flight attendants disappear to their safety seats, suitcases rattle overhead, passengers become very quiet or noisy depending on how much they get thrown around, and thoughts of *Will I survive?* fill the heads of the uninitiated. Fortunately, turbulent conditions are rare and can usually be avoided. My husband, who is a private pilot, likes to remind me that turbulence is like driving on a bumpy country road. The thermal pockets feel like tires jolting under loose gravel – not dangerous, just jiggly and annoying. To me, I am somewhere in between the uninitiated who worry about survival and the experienced pilot. Intellectually I know that we will most likely be fine, but I hate the big bumps that make me feel out of control.

Out of control is just how I felt for the first years after Jacob was diagnosed with schizophrenia. Taking care of myself was the last thing on my mind. What I learned, of course, was that caregivers have to do what "big people" do when airline passengers hit turbulent weather: put the oxygen mask on themselves first before helping others. Even though it sounds selfish, there is a very good reason we are given this instruction. How would a small child feel if he or she were comfortably breathing with their mask and discovered their parent was passed out in the seat next to them? I needed to be conscious and available when my son needed me in the early years.

This chapter describes several methods which I eventually used to tamp down my anguish and stress and develop balance in my own life. These ideas are not particularly novel or difficult to execute, but what is hard is making self-care a priority when you need it the most. I recall a time in the swirl of anguish when Jacob was close to graduating from college, but he also wanted to move out and leave the structure of our home that had been so essential to his schoolwork. It seemed like a terrible decision and would most likely keep him from graduating that semester. I was probably yelling loud enough for everyone to hear for blocks away, and Jacob just looked at me calmly and said, "Mom, are you still meditating?"

Certainly, as a psychologist, I had learned ways to deal with stress, including various ways to meditate. Teaching stress-management techniques to my clients was an important and a frequent occurrence. From my own line of work, I already knew that stress affects healthy behaviors and choices, such as how much sleep a person gets or what foods they eat. Eventually, high levels of stress reduce the immune system's ability to ward off illness and take care of itself (Kiecolt-Glaser & Glaser).

Despite this knowledge, when my personal world began to tumble and go belly up, I felt that all I could do was tread water. During these more challenging times my needs took a back seat, not because I wanted to be a martyr, but because they were just not a top priority. My life seemed to be in a constant state of upheaval. I continued to work, do things for my daughter who was still in high school, occasionally babysit our two step-grandchildren who were born at that time, try to enjoy the first few years of a new marriage, and manage the turmoil of helping Jacob find a balance regarding treatment, school and life in general. Most of the details of events during that time are a blur, however. This was a time mainly characterized by stress, sadness and insomnia.

A friend of mine whose sister has schizophrenia believed that her mother's health deteriorated because of the stress caused by her daughter's illness. Her greatest challenges throughout her daughter's life post-diagnosis were the heartbreaking attempts to get her daughter the treatment she needed. Most of the time her sister did not believe she needed help. Navigating the process of recovery with your son or daughter can be immensely challenging, and caregivers can be at risk for health problems due to stress (Moudatasou et al, 2021, Family Caregiver Alliance, 2006, and Evercare et al, 2006). How I was handling my stress was bound to affect my health too. Jacob's response to my frantic yelling was a wake-up call. I needed to get busy and develop an action plan that made me a useful advocate for him rather than an emotional basket case!

My first step was to resume my former routines. For many years I engaged in a 20-minute focused transcendental meditation once or twice a day. In the past, that was probably my most effective way of maintaining calmness and control in my life. Later, as a single parent for seven or eight years, I was lucky to get in a single session. This practice can be helpful even once a day. A focused meditation using a repeated calming word as a mantra (i.e., "relax", "peaceful", "serene", etc.) or a visual image representing peacefulness (i.e., walking on a beach) slows down your body, increases calming brainwaves, and gives you special time in a busy day to take care of yourself physically and emotionally (Horowitz, 2010).

A lot of people try meditation but give up because they find that their thoughts stray too much, especially when they are under a lot of pressure. The ironic truth is that wandering thoughts are a normal part of the meditation process. Becoming aware of these distractions and gently bringing your thoughts back to the mantra or image is the magic of meditation. In fact, when you accept your mind-wandering as normal and don't get upset when it happens, you may find that each time you return to the focus you experience even more calmness.

The next step was to think back to other times in my life when I had experienced unusual amounts of stress and what I did to survive. I easily identified graduate school as a time when I was juggling work, classes and dissertation writing. Looking back, that seems like a piece of cake compared to what was happening now with my son's illness. During those days I began practicing yoga in addition to meditation. I bicycled every week to a yoga class near campus and immersed myself in the calming movements and breathing exercises led by a very good teacher.

While bicycling to yoga classes wasn't so convenient anymore, I did order some good DVDs, and now there are many websites and YouTube channels available too. With the help of the videos, I added yoga to my stress-management routine in the comfort of my home. When working, I did my best to get up earlier than usual to do sunrise yoga. Even now, after retirement, yoga mornings provide a peaceful way to start the day. Since it has become such an important part of my routine, I created a special space in my house devoted to meditation and yoga. The view from the window in this space affords a view of cherry tree branches that change with the season, our backyard with two busy bird feeders, and our vegetable and herb garden. Lighting a candle with a calming scent at the beginning of my practice enhances the relaxing setting. At the end of my favorite DVD, the teacher encourages her students to recognize how good it feels to take this special time for yourself.

You are going to think I went overboard when you hear that I also added 30 minutes of aerobic walking to this self-care routine. Walking also provides energy as well as time to think about other things besides worries. When walking outside, I can enjoy the birds singing, the flowers blooming, the blueness or greyness of the sky, and remember that there is a bigger world with larger patterns of life than my own little circle. Stress-management literature addresses the need for people to get outside and enjoy nature. There, I can put my thoughts and concerns into a bigger picture. If the weather is bad, using the treadmill and watching something on Comedy Central, a funny program or something that is engaging can transport me elsewhere too. Walking, either indoors or out, has become another important resource for self-care (Wei et al, 2006).

Truthfully, laughing was not at the top of my list during those early years, but research does support the benefits of laughter for managing stress. It releases endorphins that help to counteract negative emotions and feelings and can give a boost to the immune system (Mora-Ripoli, 2010). Some experts believe that 90 percent of all illnesses are stress-related. While the relationship between your mind – how you think and feel – and your body is complicated and sometimes difficult to research, there is a significant amount of literature supporting the importance of thoughts and emotions mediating stress responses. How we respond to stressful events can have a direct impact on our physical health.

A life-changing story about Norman Cousins, who was the editor of *Saturday Review* for many years, illustrates the power of our mind-body connection. In 1964 he was diagnosed with a painful, serious illness affecting his connective tissues. His chances of recovery were 1 in 500. He decided that his pain medications were only making him feel worse, so he checked himself out of the hospital and went to a motel to begin a self-prescribed regimen of laughter therapy. He proceeded to read funny books and jokes and watch movies and TV shows that made him laugh heartily. As time went on, his pain lessened, he was able to sleep better, and he managed to live until 1990.

Laughter worked for him and I find it often works for me. I almost always feel better when I can laugh out loud. Like walking outside, it gives a different perspective on life. Seeing the bigger picture helps to deal with the nitty gritty of caregiving and provides much-needed balance.

As a psychologist who often used Cognitive Behavior Therapy and hypnosis as interventions, I have a great respect for the power of words. What we say to ourselves, our self-talk, and the words that we use to describe situations or events can increase or decrease the intensity of stress in our lives. If, for instance, I say (or think) to myself, "This diagnosis is terrible. My son is never going to get better. We might as well give up," I most likely will feel powerless and depressed. However, if instead I say, "This diagnosis is pretty bad. I need to find out how other individuals have coped and what is the best treatment for Jacob," I can lessen the feeling of powerlessness. I may not feel elated, but having a plan is a lot more hopeful. I may not have any control over whether Jacob has schizophrenia, but I can control how I view it or what I think about it. What we say to ourselves and what we spend time thinking about often determines our emotions and moods.

This is not the power of positive thinking exactly, and is not meant to imply that thinking everything is rosy will make it so.

Unfortunately, a parent can't wish or think away their child's schizophrenia. Believing reality is important, but reality can consist of the good, the bad and the in-betweens. Perhaps you have seen those ambiguous pictures that can be seen in two or three different ways i.e., the old woman and the young woman or the stemmed vase and two faces looking at each other. These pictures illustrate how there can be more than one way to look at most every situation. Even witnesses to an automobile accident often see very different details. In other words, what we choose as a focus can increase or decrease our ability to manage stress.

Of course, in reality, I often became discouraged, upset or angry about what was happening to Jacob. It would have been easy to stay stuck in that thinking, but another option was to celebrate his up times and focus on his progress, which was also a reality as well. When feeling discouraged, I would try to look at what positive changes he had made, whether they were little improvements or big leaps. Something as minor as a haircut or a happy, confident smile could be a celebration as well as something big like a medication change that reduced auditory hallucinations. Looking for hopeful directions, possibilities, strategies yet to try and research that continued to advance treatment and recovery lessened my anguish.

Over the years he has exhibited patterns that are now recognizable, such as when he withdraws from our relationship or struggles with life events or shifts in routine. Now, though, it is easier to trust that these tough times will be met with more positive changes down the road. His illness and symptoms have changed dramatically since his initial diagnosis and his early years when he had more active hallucinations. Does he still need my guidance? Yes, but in more subtle ways. Now it's more about fine-tuning, like clothes and grooming decisions, or trying to stay awake at family events – things that ten years ago would have been at the bottom of the list. Even these behaviors have improved in the past year, and these kinds of reminders reduce my present stress level. If only I had known that the future held such promise 20 years ago! It has also been reassuring to remind myself of his many strengths that helped him through each phase of his illness and trusting that he now has the resources and support to figure out challenges that he may face. This stress-reducing perspective comes from hindsight, but has been very useful when something stressful pops up in the present. It's the hope that "this too shall pass", and trusting in the process of change and recovery.

Social support was and continues to be another good resource to deal with stress. Talking with my "saintly" husband (his words) and with family and friends was priceless. They could understand and give useful advice when needed. Most of the time my husband and I were of the same mind, and when we were not, I tried to listen with an open mind. Fortunately, my husband respected my independence as a parent and knew that, in the end, I would probably be the decision-maker with regard to my son. He was much more objective about problematic situations and he helped me sort through decisions from a less emotional view.

As mentioned earlier, we did sometimes reverse roles. There were times when he was more empathetic and I was more hard-nosed, and vice versa. We did usually balance our interventions, though. For example, a couple of years ago we worked out an arrangement with Jacob and his wife to help them find a home and become more financially independent at the same time. The deal was that if they could manage financially without a rescue for 12 months and have some savings, I would be willing to give them a down payment. Into the third month, they ran short of food money two days before payday. Glen was all for helping them but I did not want to ruin their record. His empathy allowed me to come up with a minimal food loan that would be manageable to repay. Perhaps initially setting short-term goals would have been more realistic, but with some adjustments along the way, they successfully met their goal. Being able to bounce ideas around with Glen made problem-solving so much easier. Christina Maslach (2017), who has written much about stress management and burnout, has found that venting your frustrations with friends or family may not be helpful if that is all you do. Just venting can keep you stuck or increase your focus on frustrations and obstacles; venting needs to be followed by problem-solving. That's what my husband and I tried to do.

Finding support groups outside of the family was helpful as well, and these also had a problem-solving component. NAMI support groups could be both understanding and insightful and, while not a group experience, individual psychotherapy for myself during the second or third year of Jacob's illness helped me to deal with my personal issues related to grief, guilt and moving forward. In addition, it was important to help my son find mental health professionals who were willing to sometimes include family as part of the treatment team.

Slowly, my social network began to grow. As I became braver about sharing my experiences with friends and colleagues, I discovered how many other people have been impacted by schizophrenia or another serious mental illness. Many either had a loved one with this diagnosis or a similar disability of some sort. That is how I found out about a close friend's sister. Later, an acquaintance at my new church disclosed that she married a man with schizophrenia. One of my best friends from high school thought her nephew had the illness. Another friend from college recently wrote that one of her friends' sons struggles with schizophrenia, and once, when getting a routine mammogram, I shared something about Jacob with the nurse and she said her daughter had it too. A similar experience happened later at a community meeting when I spoke of my desire to write this book. Numerous clients had parents or relatives with the disease. Of course, client relationships are not two-way, but still hearing their stories was interesting and helped me feel less isolated. Discovering support in so many different places was amazing. It has been especially interesting to hear the stories of others.

Reading and learning as much as I could about schizophrenia was also very useful. I found many good self-help books and professional research as well. Stress often increases when you find that you are losing control of your life. Becoming more knowledgeable and finding out what could be done to help Jacob increased my sense of control. Knowing how the illness unfolds, understanding the available treatments, finding out what does and doesn't usually work, and discovering strategies to cope with new or continuing issues increased my ability to respond in a positive way. Expanding my choices was empowering. Purging my bookshelves of the former ideas that schizophrenia was a hopeless diagnosis only added to that feeling!

In addition, reading just for fun offered an escape that could transport my thoughts to another setting. Reading about people who have managed to survive – historical fiction and biographies of strong women especially – has been uplifting. Both allowed my mind a rest and were inspiring. Eleanor Roosevelt, Malala Yousafzai and Mother Teresa top the list as models for resiliency and courage. Not that I would ever compare myself with such gifted and high achievers, but their ability to transcend challenges and achieve the seemingly impossible gave me hope that I could cope and make a difference in my own way. Their stories are reminders that life is not necessarily easy or rosy, but it can be manageable.

Cooking and baking were other go-to stress management activities for me. I remember Bree in *Desperate Housewives* who loved to bake and finally started her own catering business. When she experienced a lot of stress, which was frequently in that series, she would find her way to her kitchen to bake pies until she had created the perfect one. In one scene she whipped up at least 20 apple pies until she finally made one that met her standards. She rationalized her obsession with the thought that when everything in your life is falling apart, you can take control by making the perfect pie. While my culinary skills were far from perfect, nor would they ever have made day-job money, I did feel a sense of control when I followed a recipe or created something on my own. For me, and probably for Brie, I guess, it was the concreteness of cooking that made order out of the chaos. Structure and consistency can be calming and soothing as well.

Praying a lot has also helped. This is not research speaking, but it is based on my own experience. My faith in God has deepened following moments of great doubt and anger. Of course, I am a fickle human who wonders if I am praying for no reason, but then I am put to shame for my incredible doubts. Sometimes there just is no other way to explain how things seem to work the way they do without providential intervention. I pray for Jacob's happiness, recovery and independence every day, even when my doubts are overwhelming.

What seems to happen is that his setbacks turn around. Problems do get resolved. He figures things out, I find resources, and we all find ways to keep on making it work. As much as he and I both actively seek solutions, sometimes there can be no other explanation than God answering my prayers.

Going to work and having to get outside my own thoughts helped immensely too. As a psychologist, focusing on my patients and their problems and needs provided perspective. Knowing that other people also struggled and made it through tough times or difficult experiences was reassuring. But even if I had not been a psychologist or working in a helping profession, having a career or job commitments provides an opportunity to step into a different space and interact with those beyond your inner circle – and your immediate problems. Taking a break from my own ruminations and problem-solving was refreshing. Walking away, so to speak, gave me the opportunity to return with new vision.

This chapter would not be complete without talking about grasshoppers and my favorite stress-management technique. It was during this process of sharing my experience with others that I developed one of my best friendships. Marie and I had already known each other professionally for many years, but we began to talk more openly at a memorial service for a mutual friend. It was then that she disclosed that her sister was diagnosed with schizophrenia many years ago. During the memorial service, one of the speakers described our mutual friend as a grasshopper rather than an ant. He further explained that ants keep their noses to the grindstone and constantly work. Life is always very busy and serious for ants. He thought our deceased friend was more of a grasshopper. Though she worked and did her job well, she also knew how to hop around, travel, have adventures and make time for fun. He was right. She loved to take off on trips with friends, throw good parties and just enjoy life. She filled her life with adventure and yet she had a successful career as well.

This metaphor inspired Marie and me to be part-time grasshoppers. At the reception following the service, we began to schedule what we called "Grasshopper Days" for ourselves. We picked one Friday each month to be client-free and plan a fun excursion – hiking, shopping, seeing a movie, exploring a nearby area of the city, making bread or whatever else we decided. These days were special and helpful, and allowed us to get in touch with a younger, more carefree part of ourselves. I am sure it was good for us to take a break from work and from caregiver pressure, too.

Being a grasshopper and nurturing the happy-go-lucky parts of myself was essential, whether I had a family member with schizophrenic symptoms or not. But since that was the case, it was certainly healing to release the "grasshopper" within me. Taking this needed time for escape, silliness, laughter and fun was a way of putting the oxygen mask on myself first and staying healthy. After all, a healthy caregiver is not only a happier person, but a better support to those who rely on them.

CHAPTER 13

WHAT'S NEXT?

This is not the end of the story. Rather, it is the beginning of another phase of the recovery process – reaching out to others and sharing our experiences. I wrote this book with Jacob's assistance as a way to help others who are going through similar circumstances. This is not a guidebook, but rather an illustration of how schizophrenia can impact lives in the 21st century and how we coped with it.

During our 20-year journey, we have gleaned some key factors that facilitated my son's progress. After writing this book, Jacob and I discussed what were the most helpful interventions for his recovery. Some of these key factors are described in more detail in Chapter 9. It is important to remember that recovery factors vary from one individual to another but many of these ideas could be helpful to other families. What we learned about his recovery during this time is summarized below, not necessarily in order of importance:

1. Early identification of his symptoms led to timely treatment. His own recognition and desire for treatment added to the success of early interventions.

2. His willingness to try new medications was important. Even now his treatment may still need to be tweaked due to side effects that can develop after prolonged use or because of the discovery of a formula that is even better.

3. Medication compliance is another important factor. Jacob has been consistent with his prescriptions so that facilitated his treatment

progress. While injectable medications are available, that is a decision that we never had to face. Jacob wants and trusts his treatment and his medical providers.

4. Another factor that contributed to his recovery is the fact that he does not use alcohol or street drugs, as substance abuse complicates recovery. Dual treatment programs are available for individuals with schizophrenia and substance abuse issues, but Jacob has stayed clear of this complication.

5. It has been critical to keep a timeline of his treatment, which includes doctors and therapists, medications, results of these prescriptions and significant events in his life. Sharing this information with his treatment team has facilitated transitions to new practitioners over the years.

6. For the most part, I was able to give Jacob a sense of consistency and sameness even though his world was spiraling out of control. Having a routine and direction can be calming. He continued to move toward his pre-diagnosis goals and found a sense of structure in his daily regimen. He still maintains a consistent schedule most of the time.

7. Family involvement in treatment and in his life in general helped him navigate the medical and psychological world and, hopefully, sent a message of caring and support to him as well.

8. Jacob had good medical and psychological care. The psychologist who diagnosed him with schizophrenia gave him invaluable support at the beginning. The psychiatrist who helped him find the initial medication that enabled him to start college was also especially competent. We had very few negative treatment experiences. During those early years, I worked hard to find good practitioners. Now he is able to seek out quality care for himself.

9. Jacob wants to make sure that I give credit to the power of music in his recovery process. Early on, when his voices were not tamed, he relied on music to block out their interference. He would listen to a classical radio station whenever he could in order to help him focus when talking to other people or when studying. An iPod eventually gave him more flexibility to listen wherever he might be – in class, at campus meetings or with friends and family.

Now his phone with a Bluetooth attachment is still a staple. Although his voices are not so noticeable to him, the music still provides comfort and facilitates his focus.

10. Jacob was surrounded with good academic support. Being open and asking for help and accommodations paid off. Initially his high school teachers reacted to his diagnosis with empathy and encouragement. In college, the student disability services were top-notch. His mentors were engaged in his progress. The staff and the other students who were part of the program provided support on campus when he needed it. Jacob still feels especially indebted to his history advisor.

11. My husband and I were grateful to the resources that we found. The Family-to-Family group at NAMI (www.nami.org) was the boost that we needed after Jacob's relapse, but these are other useful resources:

www.nimh.nih.gov

www.schizophrenia.com

Muesser, K T & Gingerich, S (2006). *The Complete Family Guide to Schizophrenia.* New York: The Guilford Press.

Torrey, E F (2019). *Surviving Schizophrenia.* New York: Harper Perennial.

Substance Abuse and Mental Health Services Administration (SAMHSA): 1-800- 661 HELP (4357)

findaddictionrehabs.com (for the UK)

www.nhs.uk

mentalhealth.org.uk

12. Jacob was always an active participant in his treatment. His psychiatrists and psychotherapists made sure that he was engaged in the process, and no one forced him to take medications against his will. His team listened to his needs and what he wanted to change. His experiences and his goals were their primary concern. Thanks to the Recovery to Practice movement during the past ten years or so, most patients now experience this personal respect. He is definitely the beneficiary of more advanced treatments of schizophrenia.

13. There is no doubt that living in the 21st century has increased his odds for recovery many-fold. He has been the recipient of more advanced antipsychotic medications and has worked with enlightened clinicians who value his input and recognize and build on his strengths. As statistics indicate, more and more people with schizophrenia find recovery to be an option. When expectations for recovery are part of the treatment goals, they become both hopeful and motivating to individuals with schizophrenia and to their families. We are ever so grateful to this growing body of knowledge and the evolving field of treatment for schizophrenia.

ACKNOWLEDGEMENTS

Thank you to all who have enabled this book to be published. The team at Cherish has been great, especially Kayleigh McGowan, Jess Owen, Soraya Nair and editor Victoria Godden.

Thank you to friends and colleagues. Charrie Schnieder, Ph.D., has provided valuable advice from the beginning. Lois and Mert Corwin, Jim Dahmann, Ph.D., Donna Jackson, Ph.D., Carolyn McCabe, Ph.D., Elaine Murray, Linda Rhyne, Ph.D., Carole Stokes-Brewer, Ph.D., Christy and Larry Walter, Bill Wester, Ed.D., and Lillie Weiss, Ph.D. have given needed help and encouragement.

I am grateful for family support and patience from my husband, and my daughter who kept me going even when I felt discouraged. My husband might have wished that he had better "hide-outs" in our house!

The cover photo was taken by my mother and Jacob's grandmother, who has a special place in all of our hearts.

Much credit goes to my early editors, Melinda Zemper-Gehring and Carl Tishler, Ph.D., who kept me on track with clear, useful feedback.

And, of course, a most important thank you to Jacob who agreed to share his story to help others.

REFERENCES

American Psychiatric Association (2013). *Diagnostic and Statistical Manual of Mental Disorders, Fifth Edition*. Arlington, Va. American Psychiatric Association.

American Psychological Association & Jansen, M.A. (2014, August). Recovery to Practice Initiative Curriculum: Reframing Psychology for the Emerging Health Care Environment. https://www.apa.org/pi/mfp/psychology/recovery-to-practice/index

Bark, N (2002). Did Schizophrenia Change the Course of English History? The Mental Illness of Henry VI. *Medical Hypothesis*, 59(4): 416–421. doi: 10.1016/S0306-9877(02)00145-7

Board of Governors of the Federal Reserve System (2019). *Report of the Economic Well-Being of US Households in 2018* https://www.federalreserve.gov/publications/default.htm

Brohan, E, Elgie, R, Sartorius, N, Thornicroft, G, & GAMIAN Europe Study Group (2010). Self-stigma, Empowerment and Perceived Discrimination Among People with Schizophrenia in 14 European Countries: The GAMAIN-Europe Study. *Schizophrenia Research*. doi: 10.1016/j.schres.2010.1065

Brooks, D (29 March 2019). Longing for Internet Cleanse. *The New York Times*, p. 25.

Center for Disease Control (2017). Burden of Mental Illness. https://www.cdc.gov/mentalhealth/basics/burden.htm

Cernis, E, Vassos, E, Brebion, G, McKenna, P J, Murray, R M, David, A S, & McCabe, J H (2015). Schizophrenia patients with high intelligence: A clinically distinct sub-type of schizophrenia? *European Psychiatry*, 30(5): 628–32. doi.org/10.1016/i.eurpsy.2015.02.007

Clay, R A (2014). From Serious Mental Illness to Recovery. *Monitor of Psychology*, 45(8), 54–57.

Desmarais, S L, Van Dorn, R D, Johnson, K L, Grimm, K J, Douglas, PhD & Swartz, M S (2014). Community Violence Perpetration and Victimization Among Adults with Mental Illnesses. *American Journal of Public Health*, 104 (12): 2342–2349. doi: 10.2105/ AJPH.2013.301680

Evercare & National Alliance for Caregiving (2006). *A Study of Caregivers in Decline.* Retrieved from https://www.caregiving.org/ wp-content/upload/2020/05/Caregivers-in-Decline-Study-FINAL/ lowres.pdf

Family Caregiver Alliance (2006). *Caregiver Health.* Retrieved from https://www.caregiver.org/resource/caregiver-health/#

Frese, F & Frese, P (1991). Schizophrenia: Surviving the World of Normals and A Love Story: Living with Someone with Schizophrenia (Video), Wellness Productions.

Gottesman, I I (1991). *Schizophrenia Genesis.* San Francisco: W H Freeman.

Horsselenberg, E M, Busschbach, J T, Aleman, A, Pijnenborg, G H (2016). Self-Stigma and Its Relationship with Victimization, Psychotic Symptoms and Self-Esteem among People with Schizophrenia Spectrum Disorders. *PLoS ONE*, 11(10), Article e0149763. doi.org/10.1371/journal.pone.0149763

Horowitz, S (2010). Health Benefits of Meditation: What the Newest Research Shows. *Alternative and Complementary Therapies*, 16(4): 223–228. doi: 10.1089/act.2010.16402

Huabing, L, Oiong, L, Enhua, X, Qiuyun, L, Zhong, H, & Xiong, M (February 2014). Methamphetamine Enhances the Development of Schizophrenia in First-Degree relatives of Patients with Schizophrenia. *Canadian Journal of Psychiatry*, 107–113. doi: 10.1177/070674371405900206

Kasckow, J, Felmut, K, & Zisook, S (2011). Managing Suicide Risk in Patients with Schizophrenia. *CNS Medications*, 25(2), 129–143. doi: 10.2165/11586450-000000000-00000

Kersting, K (2005). Empowering 'consumers' of treatment. *Monitor on Psychology*, 36(1): 39.

Kety, S S, Rosenthal, D, Wender, P H (1978). Genetic relationships within the schizophrenia spectrum: evidence from adoption studies. *In Critical Issues in Psychiatric Diagnoses* (eds Spitzer, R L & Klein, D F), 213–23. New York: Raven Press.

Kiecolt-Glaser, J & Glaser, R. Stress and Health Research homepage: http://pni.osumc.edu

Laing, R D (1976). *The Politics of Experience*. New York: Ballantine Books.

Lukens, E P, Thorning, H, & Lohrer, S (October 2004). Sibling Perspectives on Severe Mental Illness Reflections on Self and Family. *American Journal of Orthopsychiatry*, 74(4): 489–501. doi: 10.1037/0002-9432.74.4.489

McGinty, E E, Kennedy-Hendricks, A, Choksy, S, Barry, C L (2016). Trends I News Media Coverage of Mental Illness in The United States: 1995–2014. *Health Affairs*, 35(6): 1121–1129. doi.org/10.1377/hlthaff.2016.0011

MacKenzie, L E, Abidi, S, Fisher, H L, Propper, L, Bagnell, A, Morash-Conway, J, Glover, J M, Cumby, J, Hajek, T, Schultze-Lutter, F, Pajer, K, Alda, M & Uher, R, (January 2016). Stimulant Medication and Psychotic Symptoms in Offspring of Parents with Mental Illness. *Pediatrics*, 137(1). doi: 10.1542/peds.2015.2486

Maslach, C (2017). Finding Solutions to the Problem of Burnout. *Consulting Psychology Journal: Practice and Research*, 69(2): 143–152.

Metzl, J M & MacLeish, K T (2015). Mental Illness, Mass Shootings, and the Politics of American Firearms. *American Journal of Public Health*, 105(2): 240–249. doi: 10.2105/AJPH.2014.3022242

Moudatsou, M., Koukouli, S. Palioka, E., Pattakou, G., Teleme, P., Fasoi, G., Kaba, E. & Stavropoulou, A. (2021) Caring for Patients with Psychosis: Mental Health Professionals' Views on Informal Caregivers' Needs. International Journal of Environmental Research and Public Health.18(2). doi: 10.3390/lijerph18062964

Mora-Ripoli, R (2010). The Therapeutic Value of Laughter in Medicine. *Alternative Therapies in Health and Medicine*, 16(6): 56–64.

Mucci, A, Silvana, G, Dino, G, Rossi, A, Rocca, P, Bertolino, A, Aguglia, E, Amore, M, Bellomo, A, Blondi, M, Blasi, G, Brasso, C, Bucci, P, Carpiniello, B, Cuomo, A, Dell'Osso, L, Giordano,

G M, Marchesi, C, Monteleone, P, Niolu, C, ... Maj, M (2021). Factors Associated with Real Life Functioning in Persons with Schizophrenia in a 4-year Follow-up Study of the Italian Network for Research on Psychoses. *Journal of American Medical Association Psychiatry*. Advance online publication. https:// doi10.1001/ jamapsychiatry.2020.4614

Namade, R & Dombeck, M (2009). http://www.mentalhealth.net/ articles/prognosis-and-recovery-of-schizophrenia

National Coalition for the Homeless (2017). Mental Illness and the Homeless. http://www.nationalhomeless.org/wp-content/ uploads/2017/06/Mental-Illness-and-Homelessness.pdf

Nestor, P G (2002). Mental Disorder and Violence: Personality Dimensions and Clinical Features. https//doi.org/10.1176/appi. ajp.159.12.1973

Pardini, C (2016). ADHD in Schizophrenia patients: Recommendations for Managing a Common Comorbidity. *Monthly Prescribing Reference* https://www.empr.com/home/features/adhd-in-schizophrenia-patients-recommendations-for-managing-a-common-comorbidity/

Pescosolido, B A, Martin, J D, Long, J S, Medina, T R, Phelan, J C & Lind, B C (2010). A Disease Like Any Other? A Decade of Change in Public Reactions to Schizophrenia, Depression, and Alcohol Dependence. *American Journal of Psychiatry*, 167: 1321–30.

Peterson, J K & Densley, J A (2019). *The Violence Project Database of Mass Shootings in the United States, 1966–2019*. The Violence Project. Retrieved from https://w.ww.theviolenceproject.org.

Potts, B & Obert, K (2016). "Does Mental Illness Cause Gun Violence?" The Public's Perception Verse the Mental Ill's Reality. *OPA Review*, November/December, 13–15.

Saad, L (2019). More blaming Extremism, Heated Rhetoric for Mass Shootings. *Gallup*. https://news.gallup.com/poll/266750/ blaming-extremism-heated-rhetoric-mass-shootings.aspx

Sekas, A, Bialas, A R, de Rivera, H, Davis, A, Hammond, T R, Kamitaki, N, Tooley, K, Presumey, J, Baum, M, Van Doren, V, Genovese, G, Rose, S A, Handsaker, R E, Schizophrenia Working

Group of the Psychiatric Genomes Consortium, Daly, M, Carroll, M C, Stevens, B & McCarroll S A (2016). Schizophrenia Risk from Complex Variation of Complement Component 4. *Nature*, 3: 177–183. doi: 10.1038/nature16549

Siris, S G (2001). Suicide and Schizophrenia. *Journal of Psychopharmacology*, 15(2): 127–135. doi.org/10.1177/026988110101500209

Smerud, P E & Rosenfarb, I R (2011). The Therapeutic Alliance and Family Psychoeducation in the Treatment of Schizophrenia: An Exploratory Prospective Change Process Study. *Couple and Family Psychology, Research and Practice*, 1(5): 85–91.

Stepnicki, P, Kondej, M, & Kaczor, A A (2018). Current Concepts and Treatments of Schizophrenia. *Molecules*, 23(8): 2087. doi: 10.3390/molecules23082087

Shrivastava, A, Johnston, M, & Bureau, Y (2012). Stigma of Mental Illness – 1: Clinical reflections. *Mens Sana Monographs*, 10(1): 70–84. doi: 10.4103/0973-1229.90181

Stilo, S A & Murray, R H (2019). Non-genetic Factors in Schizophrenia. *Current Psychiatric Report*, 21(10): 100–120, doi: 1007/s11920-1019-3

Sumiyoshi, T, Higuchi, Y & Uehara, T (2013). Neural Basis for the Ability of Atypical Antipsychotic Medications to Improve Cognition in Schizophrenia. *Frontiers in Behavioral Neuroscience*, 7(140). http://doi:10.3389/frbeh.2013.00140

Swanson, J W, McGinty, E E, Fazel, S & Mays, V M (2015). Mental illness and reduction of gun violence and suicide: bringing epidemiologic research to policy. *Annul of Epidemiology*, 25(5): 366–376. doi: 10.1016/j.annepidem.2014.03.004

Torrey, E F (2019). *Surviving Schizophrenia: A Family Manual.* New York, New York: Harper Perennial.

Torrey, E F, Kennard, A D, Eslinger, D F, Biasotti, M C & Fuller, D F (2013). Justifiable homicides by Law Enforcement Officers: What is the Role of Mental Illness? Joint Report of The Treatment Advocacy Center and the National Sheriffs' Association. http://tacreports.org/storage/documents/2013-justifiable-homicedes.pdf

Wei, B, Kilpatrick, M, Naquin, M & Cole, D (2006). Psychological Perceptions to Walking, Water Aerobics, and Yoga in College Students. *American Journal of Health Studies*, 21(3/4): 142–147.

Winklbaur, B, Ebner, N, Gabriele, S, Kenneth, T, Gabriele, F (2006). Substance Abuse in Patients with Schizophrenia. *Dialogues in Clinical Neuroscience*, 8(1): 37–43. doi: 10.31887/DCNS.2006.8.1/bwinklbaur

Yalom, I D (1975). *The Basic Theory and Practice of Group Psychotherapy.* New York, New York: Basic Books, Inc. American Psychiatric Association (2013). Diagnostic and Statistical Manual of Mental Disorders, Fifth Edition. Arlington, Va. American Psychiatric Association.

ABOUT CHERISH EDITIONS

Cherish Editions is a bespoke self-publishing service for authors of mental health, wellbeing and inspirational books.

As a division of Trigger Publishing, the UK's leading independent mental health and wellbeing publisher, we are experienced in creating and selling positive, responsible, important and inspirational books, which work to de-stigmatize the issues around mental health and improve the mental health and wellbeing of those who read our titles.

Founded by Adam Shaw, a mental health advocate, author and philanthropist, and leading psychologist Lauren Callaghan, Cherish Editions aims to publish books that provide advice, support and inspiration. We nurture our authors so that their stories can unfurl on the page, helping them to share their uplifting and moving stories.

Cherish Editions is unique in that a percentage of the profits from the sale of our books goes directly to leading mental health charity Shaw Mind, to deliver its vision to provide support for those experiencing mental ill health.

Find out more about Cherish Editions by visiting cherisheditions.com or by joining us on:
Twitter @cherisheditions
Facebook @cherisheditions
Instagram @cherisheditions

Cherish
EDITIONS

ABOUT SHAWMIND

A proportion of profits from the sale of all Trigger books go to their sister charity, Shawmind, also founded by Adam Shaw and Lauren Callaghan. The charity aims to ensure that everyone has access to mental health resources whenever they need them.

You can find out more about the work Shawmind do by visiting their website: shawmind.org or joining them on:

Twitter @Shaw_Mind
Facebook @ShawmindUK
Instagram @Shaw_Mind

Your Local Mental Health & Wellbeing Charity

Lightning Source UK Ltd.
Milton Keynes UK
UKHW041844141221
395637UK00001B/33